GSK in China:

Anti-Bribery Enforcement Goes Global

By

Thomas Fox

Author's Note

The year 2013 brought the anti-corruption compliance world a new situation as the Chinese government aggressively investigated, for the first time, a western company for bribery and corruption of Chinese citizens in China, based on Chinese domestic law. The company, GlaxoSmithKline PLC (GSK), was convicted of corruption in September 2014. I wanted to put together in one volume, the background facts, information from the trials and conviction and add some of the most significant lessons to be learned for any compliance practitioner going forward. Thanks to Maurice Gilbert at Consileum Inc., and Corporate Compliance Insights (CCI) for the idea and my heart of gold wife, Michele, for editing.

Table of Contents

Author's Note 3

I. The Investigation Goes Public 5

The Timeline of Events 6

Chapter I - The First Month 7

Chapter II - GSK Prior US Enforcement Action 10

Chapter III - Some Chinese Law 13

Chapter IV - The GSK Corruption Investigation Deepens 16

Chapter V - GSK Faces a Bad Day at Black Rock 18

Chapter VI - GSK's 2001 China Bribery Scandal 20

Chapter VII - No Sex Please, We're British: The Sex Tape 22

Chapter VIII - Things Only Get Worse for GSK 24

Chapter IX - International Ripples From the Chinese Corruption Investigations 25

Chapter X - Missed Red Flags 27

Chapter XI - The Problem of Fake Invoices in China 30

II. The Convictions 32

Chapter XII - Humphrey and Wife Convicted 33

Chapter XIII - GSK Convicted 35

Chapter XIV - Some Thoughts on the Verdict 38

III. What Does It All Mean? 41

Chapter XV - What Can You Do? 42

Chapter XVI - Due Diligence and the Management of Third Parties Going Forward in China 45

Chapter XVII - Business Lessons from GSK 49

Chapter XVIII - Board of Directors and Doing Business in China 52

Chapter XIX - More Compliance Lessons 57

Chapter XX - Is a Country Sweep Coming to China? 65

Chapter XXI - One More Nail in the Coffin of a Compliance Defense 67

Chapter XXII - China and the International Fight Against Corruption 69

About the Author 72

I. The Investigation Goes Public

The Timeline of Events

GSK First Month Timeline (2013)	
June 28	Police announce they have placed GSK officials under investigation for 'economic crimes'.
July 4	July 4 - National Development and Reform Commission announces it has opened probe into costs of medicines by GSK and others.
July 7	Wall Street Journal reports internal GSK WB notified GSK back in Jan of corruption allegations.
July 11	Public Security Ministry issues statement accusing GSK of bribery. GSK claims this is 1st details it has been given of allegations.
July 15	4 senior company execs 'detained'. Finance chief barred from leaving country.
July 16	GSK General Counsel placed under 'house arrest' along with 30 other employees.
July 16	GSK China exec admits bribery on TV.
July 22	GSK 'apologizes' for breaking Chinese law.
July 26	Reported that a US national, who was investigator for GSK and his wife were detained in Shanghai.
GSK Year Two Timeline (2014)	
May	UK Serious Fraud Office and US Department of Justice announce they have opened separate investigations into GSK.
May	Chinese authorities accuse GSK China Country Manager Mark Reilly of orchestrating China bribery scheme.
June	Allegations of GSK bribery in Syria, Iraq, Poland and Greece surface. GSK China unit employees bring claims that were forced by management to pay bribes and told to lie to investigators
July	It is revealed that GSK was sent a 'sex tape' of China country manager and his girlfriend by same anonymous whistleblower who made allegations of bribery.
July	Trial of Humphrey and wife is announced.
August	One day trial held for Humphrey and wife. Both convicted.
September	GSK pleads guilty in secret one-day trial. Fined $491MM

Chapter I - The First Month

In June 2013, the Chinese government announced that it had found evidence that the UK pharmaceutical giant GlaxoSmithKline PLC (GSK) was involved in bribery and corruption of Chinese doctors. An article in the Financial Times (FT), entitled *"China accuses GSK of bribery"* by Kathrin Hille and John Aglionby, reported that "China has accused GlaxoSmithKline of being at the centre of a "huge" scheme to raise drug prices in three of the country's biggest cities and said the UK-based drugmaker's staff had confessed to bribing government officials and doctors. China's Ministry of Public Security said a probe in Changsha, Shanghai and Zhengzhou found that GSK had tried to generate sales and raise drug prices by bribing government officials, pharmaceutical industry associations and foundations, hospitals and doctors." They reported that some of the techniques used included the issuance of "fake VAT receipts and used travel agents to issue fake documents to gain cash, according to the ministry. Some executives had also taken advantage of their positions to take kickbacks from organising conferences and projects." Further, ""There are many suspects, the illegal behaviour continued over a long time and its scale is huge," the ministry said."

In another FT article, entitled *"China steps up GSK bribery probe"*, Andrew Jack and Leslie Hook reported that "The Chinese authorities have stepped up their investigation into GlaxoSmithKline accusing it of being the ringleader of a half-a-billion-dollar bribery scandal involving 700 companies." They reported on a briefing given by "Gao Feng, the lead Chinese investigator on a probe into the UK drugs group, said police were examining Rmb3bn ($488m) in deals from as far back as 2007. Chinese police believe that GSK used travel agencies and consultancies as a conduit to bribe doctors and lawyers in order to boost sales and profits."

In an article in the Wall Street Journal (WSJ), entitled *"China Drops Hammer on Glaxo"*, Laurie Burkitt and Christopher M. Matthews reported on a televised interview of Liang Hong, the GSK China Vice President and Operations Manager, where he "described for viewers of China Central Television how staffers would allegedly organize conferences that never happened and divert the money to bribe government officials, hospitals and medical personnel to get them to use Glaxo's products." He was quoted as saying, "Dealing with some government departments requires some money that couldn't be claimed normally under company expenses." Burkitt and Matthews said that "The broadcast follows detailed allegations by China's Ministry of Public Security on Monday accusing Glaxo of using travel agencies as vehicles to bribe hospitals, officials and medical personnel to sell more drugs at inflated prices. Officials also alleged the travel agencies offered what the officials called sexual bribes to Glaxo executives to keep company business."

These findings flew in the face of the company's own internal investigation into allegations of bribery and corruption brought by a whistleblower. Hille and Aglionby reported that "GSK said it had conducted an internal four-month investigation after a tip-off that staff had bribed doctors to issue prescriptions for its drugs. The internal inquiry found no evidence of wrongdoing, it said." Indeed after the release of information from the Chinese government, which GSK said was the first it had heard of the investigation, it released a statement quoted in the FT article, which stated ""We continuously monitor our businesses to ensure they meet our strict compliance procedures – we have done this in China and found no evidence of bribery or corruption of doctors or government officials. However, if evidence of such activity is provided we will act swiftly on it," the company said."

In another FT article, by Hook and Jack entitled "*GSK is test case in China's rules laboratory*", they noted that GSK had received information from an internal whistleblower back in January. The company investigated claims of bribery and corruption and publicly announced that the company had found no such evidence of "bribery or corruption in relation to our sales and marketing…in China". Further, the company claimed it was unaware of any allegations of bribery of doctors to prescribe its drugs until there was a public announcement by China's Public Security Ministry.

Unfortunately for GSK, not only did the Chinese government uncover evidence of bribery and corruption, such information was viewed and reported on by the WSJ. Laurie Burkitt, in an article entitled "*China Accuses Glaxco of Bribes*", wrote that "Emails and documents reviewed by the Journal discuss a marketing strategy for Botox that targeted 48 doctors and planned to reward them with either a percentage of the cash value of the prescription or educational credits, based on the number of prescriptions the doctors made. The strategy was called "*Vasily,*" borrowing its name from Vasily Zaytsev, a noted Russian sniper during World War II, according to a 2013 PowerPoint presentation reviewed by the Journal." Burkitt reported in her article that "A Glaxo spokesman has said the company probed the Vasily program and "[the] investigation has found that while the proposal didn't contain anything untoward, the program was never implemented."

Burkitt also reported that the Chinese crackdown may be a part of a larger crackdown on bribery and corruption. While it is not clear at this point, she stated that "scrutiny of foreign corporations operating in China has been heightened in recent months, as the government has launched a campaign to clean up its commercial sector, cracking down on practices authorities view as abusive or anticompetitive." In an FT article, entitled "*GSK claims show frailty of Chinese system*", Andrew Jack said that "The Chinese government has been clamping down on such practices [bribery and corruption] and attempting to keep a lid on drug costs, with an increasing focus on multinational companies. The National Development and Reform Commission in Beijing last week signaled that it was examining pricing by 60 companies."

Initially, GSK seemed to waiver on making any statement about the allegations against it. When the Chinese investigation was originally announced, the company said in a statement that "These allegations are shameful and we regret this has occurred. We are deeply concerned and disappointed by these serious allegations of fraudulent behaviour and ethical misconduct by certain individuals at the company and third-party agencies." However, by July 22, 2013, GSK's tune seemed to have changed. In a post in the FCPA Blog, entitled "*GSK apologizes for breaking China law*", Dick Cassin reported that "Abbas Hussain, the head of emerging markets for the U.K.-based drug maker, said 'Certain senior executives of GSK China, who know our systems well, appear to have acted outside of our processes and controls which breaches Chinese law.'" But it turned out that things only got worse for GSK, much worse.

Chapter II - GSK Prior US Enforcement Action

All of the above is pretty eye popping in and of itself. But consider the following about GSK, a little over one year ago, in July of 2012; GSK pled guilty and paid $3 *billion* to resolve fraud allegations and failure to report safety data in what the US Department of Justice (DOJ) called the "largest health care fraud settlement in U.S. history" according to its press release. The DOJ press release went on to state that "GSK agreed to plead guilty and to pay $3 billion to resolve its criminal and civil liability arising from the company's unlawful promotion of certain prescription drugs, its failure to report certain safety data, and its civil liability for alleged false price reporting practices." The press release noted that the resolution was the largest health care fraud settlement in US history and the largest payment ever by a drug company for legal violations.

As a part of the agreement, GSK agreed to plead guilty to a three-count criminal information, including two counts of introducing misbranded drugs, Paxil and Wellbutrin, into interstate commerce and one count of failing to report safety data about the drug Avandia to the Food and Drug Administration (FDA). Under the terms of the plea agreement, GSK paid a total of $1 billion, including a criminal fine of $956,814,400 and forfeiture in the amount of $43,185,600. GSK also paid $2 billion to resolve its civil liabilities with the federal government under the False Claims Act, based on a whistleblower's allegations. The civil settlement resolved claims relating to GSK's drugs Paxil, Wellbutrin and Avandia, additional drugs, and pricing fraud allegations.

The criminal plea agreement also included certain non-monetary compliance commitments and certifications by GSK's US president and Board of Directors, which specifically included an executed five-year Corporate Integrity Agreement (CIA) with the Department of Health and Human Services, Office of Inspector General. The plea agreement and CIA included provisions which required that GSK implement and/or maintain major changes to the way it does business, including changing the way its sales force is compensated to remove compensation based on sales goals for territories, one of the driving forces behind much of the conduct at issue in the prior enforcement action. Under the CIA, GSK is required to change its executive compensation program to permit the company to recoup annual bonuses and long-term incentives from covered executives if they or their subordinates, engaged in significant misconduct. GSK may recoup monies from executives who are current employees and those who have left the company. Additionally, the CIA also required GSK to implement and maintain transparency in its research practices and publication policies and to follow specified policies in its contracts with various health care payors.

The importance of the CIA for this anti-corruption investigation is that the CIA not only applied to the specific pharmaceutical regulations that GSK violated but all of the GSK compliance obligations, including the Foreign Corrupt Practices Act (FCPA). In addition to requiring a full and complete compliance program, the CIA specified that the company would have a

Compliance Committee, to include the Compliance Officer and other members of senior management necessary to meet the requirements of the CIA; the Compliance Committee's job was to oversee full implementation of the CIA and all compliance functions at the company. These additional functions required a Deputy Compliance Officer for each commercial business unit, Integrity Champions within each business unit and management accountability and certifications from each business unit. Training of GSK employees was specified as a key component. Further, the CIA specifically states that all compliance obligations be applied to "contractors, subcontractors, agents and other persons (including, but not limited to, third party vendors)".

GSK's Code of Conduct (entitled "*One Company One Approach*") states quite clearly, "The GSK attitude towards corruption in all its forms is simple: it is one of zero tolerance, whether committed by GSK employees, officers, complementary workforce or third parties acting for or on behalf of the company. Accordingly, we must never make, offer to make, or authorise any improper payments or provide anything of value to any individual, or at the request of any individual, for the purpose of influencing, inducing or rewarding any act, omission or decision to secure an improper advantage, or obtain and retain business."

In its Code of Practice for Promotions and Customer Interactions, there is a detailed procedure laid out for any sponsorship of a corporate event, conference or travel. This procedure requires that "The Scientific Engagement Operating Practice "Congress Sponsorships" must be followed for sponsorships of scientific and medical congresses (conferences) at international and local (country) levels". Further, if there is a grant a specific procedure must be followed.

Additionally GSK has a Third Party Code of Conduct, which states:

Third Parties shall conduct their business in an ethical manner and act with integrity. The ethics elements include the following statement:

1. **Business Integrity, Reputation and Fair Competition**
   Corruption, extortion and embezzlement are prohibited. Third Parties shall not pay or accept bribes or participate in other illegal inducements in business or government relationships.

   Third Parties should never communicate externally about GSK's prospects, performance or policies nor disclose inside Information which would affect the price of GSK securities without proper authority. Third Parties are forbidden from making any public posting of confidential or proprietary information related to any aspect of GSK's business.

   Third Parties shall conduct their business consistent with fair and vigorous competition and in compliance with all applicable anti-trust laws. Third Parties must strictly adhere to the letter and spirit of the Competition laws in all jurisdictions. Third Parties shall employ fair business practices including accurate and truthful advertising.

According to the GSK Code of Conduct, all of this is to be backed up by "a Global Ethics & Compliance team which is responsible for providing oversight and guidance to ensure compliance with applicable laws, regulations, and company policies, as well as fostering a positive, ethical work environment for all employees." The Code also states that "GSK has an active system of internal management controls to identify company risks, issues and incidents with appropriate corrective actions taken. Our Risk Management and Compliance Policy provides the framework for these internal controls, to ensure significant risks are escalated to the proper levels of senior management."

Frankly I do not know how much clearer a company can *state* that it will not engage in bribery and corruption. But the problem for GSK seems to be that none of the above was effective because the company did not follow its own stated protocols regarding its operations in China. You would think that any company which has paid *$3 billion* in fines and penalties for fraudulent actions and is under a five-year agreement to do business within the compliance laws would take all steps possible not to engage in bribery and corruption.

Chapter III - Some Chinese Law

In a FT article, entitled *"China dream sours for foreign companies"*, Tom Mitchell wrote that "The "Chinese dream" articulated by China's new president, Xi Jinping, is fast becoming a nightmare for some of the world's most powerful corporations." This is because "since then, government investigations and state media exposés targeting foreign investors have become a regular feature of the country's business landscape." Mitchell reported that some western executives "complain that foreign groups appear to be encountering particularly heavy scrutiny under the new leadership." That complaint might certainly be considered by GSK as they have become the poster child for Chinese enforcement of its own internal anti-bribery legislation.

One of the things that compliance practitioners should not lose sight of in the ongoing bribery and corruption investigation of GSK is that the investigation, detentions and arrests all involve allegations of violations of *Chinese* law, not the FCPA or UK Bribery Act. And while prosecution and even indictment or arrest under the FCPA or Bribery Act could not be termed a pleasant experience, I am relatively certain that it would pale in comparison to indictment or arrest under the applicable Chinese law prohibiting bribery of Chinese officials.

But what is the Chinese law regarding bribery and corruption of Chinese officials inside of China and what might that portend for US, UK or other western companies doing business in China? In a 2013 client alert, entitled *"Recent Developments in Chinese Antibribery Laws and Enforcement"*, the law firm of Akin Gump Strauss Hauer & Feld LLP, wrote that "The recent, very public crackdowns against alleged bribery activities by foreign firms, however, should be seen in a broader historical context and as a manifestation of developments in the legal arena that have been taking place over some time." This is because Chinese officials had previously focused on prosecution of bribe recipients, not the bribe payers. They noted that "Chinese laws against bribery can be found in the PRC Criminal Law, first promulgated in 1997. Importantly, in contrast to bribery laws in many other jurisdictions, the Chinese law applies only to the actual giving of a bribe, not to the offering of one; there is no law against attempted bribery in China. In contrast to the FCPA, the rules in China apply to bribing private individuals and entities, not just government officials."

The client alert also reported that that the Interpretations on Several Issues Concerning the Application of the Law in the Handling of Criminal Bribe-Giving Cases, adopted jointly by the Supreme People's Court and the Supreme People's Procuratorate in December 2012, which became effective in January 2013, defined more clearly the various levels of bribery, issues regarding the amount of money involved, the identity of the recipient and penalties. Additionally, it noted that "Various Chinese court rulings provide some guidance on the issue; per these rulings, the following factors are key: (i) the nature and history of the relationship between the parties; (ii) the value of the gift; (iii) the purpose and timing of the gift relative to what is obtained; and (iv) to what extent the recipient has used his or her position to promote the interests of the gift giver." However, and perhaps more ominously, the client alert also said that "given the general nature of these guidelines, prosecutors and judges have considerable discretion in determining whether a particular act amounts to an illegal bribe."

A. Penalties Under Chinese Law

Helen Zhang, Partner in the Shanghai office of the Zhong Lun Law Firm, in a presentation entitled *"Management of Corruption Exposure Legal Framework & Company Approaches"*, detailed the legal framework on Chinese anti-corruption laws. Under the criminal proceedings section, the definition of what might constitute a bribe can include "money, property, material object or interest on property that can be counted by money, such as providing house renovation, membership card containing money, token card (coupon), traveling expenses, etc., or anything of a property nature." In the administrative proceedings, there can be prosecutions for "any incorrectly recorded sales discounts or rebates" and there are several tests on what might constitute a legitimate gift, contrasting it with indicia of bribery. They include the following:

- the transaction background, such as whether the transaction parties are relatives or friends and the circumstances and degree of communications between the transaction parties in history;
- value of the money or property transacted;
- cause, time and manner of the transaction, and whether the person offering money or property has brought forward any request towards the recipient in connection with the recipient's duties; and finally
- whether the recipient secures benefits for the provider by taking advantage of his duties.

B. Defenses Available

There are defenses available to rebut allegations of bribery, pursuant to the PRC Supreme Court's interpretation, which states "if the company adopts a collective decision or the in-charge manager of the company makes a decision to voluntarily confess the bribery activities before being pursued, the penalties on the company and its relevant responsible persons can be reduced or even exempted." Further, Zhang noted that there are additional defenses available. Under general Chinese law, these are voluntary confessions and contributions to other enforcement actions and other defenses specific to bribery cases which include "blackmailed bribery and no improper interest involved".

Facilitation payments are not excluded or exempted from the Chinese bribery statutes, as facilitation payments may be deemed bribery if the facilitation of the relevant government procedures constitutes an "improper interest acquired by the briber. Pursuant to the judicial interpretations of the PRC Supreme People's Court, any attempt to obtain advantage of competition inconsistent with the principle of fair and just may also be deemed a kind of "improper interest"." Most relevant to the GSK matter, "Indirect payment of bribes through an

14

intermediary is not a defense and both the intermediary and the briber may be criminally prosecuted: (a) if the intermediary introduces the briber to a public official, he may be prosecuted for the "crime of introduction of bribery"; or (b) if the intermediary assists in the payment of bribes for the briber, he may be prosecuted for the "crime of bribery" as an accomplice of the briber."

The Akin Gump client alert ended with "For many years, U.S. companies doing business in China have had to concern themselves only with the strictures of the FCPA. The recent developments in anti-bribery enforcement in China will add to those burdens. While the FCPA and Chinese anti-bribery laws are similar in many respects, they are not identical. For example, as noted above, the FCPA applies only to bribery involving government officials; the Chinese law is not so limited. Furthermore, the FCPA contains an exception for "facilitation payments," while the Chinese law contains no such express exception. Effective compliance programs for U.S. firms operating in China will therefore need to take account of, and address, both sets of laws."

Chapter IV - The GSK Corruption Investigation Deepens

In May, 2014 the UK Serious Fraud Office (SFO) announced that it had "opened a criminal investigation into the commercial practices of GlaxoSmithKline plc and its subsidiaries." In the same Press Release the SFO said, "Whistleblowers are valuable sources of information to the SFO in its cases. We welcome approaches from anyone with inside information on all our cases including this one - we can be contacted through our secure and confidential reporting channel, which can be accessed via the SFO website." It then proceeded to provide the SFO's secure reporting website.

In a New York Times (NYT) article, entitled "*GlaxoSmithKline Under Investigation by Serious Fraud Office*", Chad Bray reported that the SFO "is investigating Glaxo's business activities in "multiple jurisdictions," according to a person familiar with the investigation who was not authorized to speak publicly." Further, "Chinese authorities have been investigating the drugmaker's business practices related to payments to doctors and other health care professionals since last year and questions have been raised in recent months about the company's practices in Iraq and Poland."

James Titcomb, reporting in The Telegraph, in an article entitled "*SFO opens criminal investigation into GlaxoSmithKline*", went further when he noted that GSK has been in contact with the SFO "in recent months in the wake of claims that it funnelled hundreds of millions of pounds to doctors and officials in countries around the globe to boost sales of its drugs." Moreover, "Chinese police have accused the company of dispensing 3bn yuan (£285m) in bribes under the leadership Mark Reilly, the former head of its Chinese business. Authorities in the country say the bribes resulted in billions of pounds in "illegal revenue" for the company."

On the Chinese side of the investigation, the NYT article reported that during the month of May, "Chinese authorities accused Mark Reilly, the former head of Glaxo's operations in China, of ordering employees to bribe doctors and other hospital staff to use the drug maker's products, resulting in more than $150 million in illegal revenue. Two other Chinese-born Glaxo executives were also charged in the matter."

When news of the Chinese investigation broke last summer, GSK claimed that "Certain senior executives of GSK China who know our systems well, appear to have acted outside of our processes and controls which breaches Chinese law," Glaxo said in July, after meeting with the Chinese authorities. "We have zero tolerance for any behavior of this nature." The Chinese authorities did not fall for this age-old attempt at corporate misdirection. Andrew Ward, reporting in a FT article entitled "*SFO opens criminal inquiry into GSK*", said that the Chinese authorities had engaged in a "ten-month investigation" which had identified 46 current or former GSK employees as "suspects".

Where were the DOJ or Securities and Exchange Commission (SEC) on these issues as they might relate to violations of the FCPA? You will recall that in July of 2012 GSK pled guilty and paid $3 billion to resolve fraud allegations and failure to report safety data in what the DOJ called the "largest health care fraud settlement in U.S. history" according to its press release.

You would think that any company that has paid $3 billion in fines and penalties for fraudulent actions would take all steps possible not to engage in bribery and corruption. Indeed as part of the settlement GSK agreed to a CIA, which not only applied to the specific pharmaceutical regulations that GSK violated but all of the GSK compliance obligations, including the FCPA.

GSK has often and very publicly stated that it was fully cooperating with all of the various investigations into its alleged bribery and corruption. Further, as reported in Ward's FT article, "GSK said it was "committed to operating its business to the highest ethical standards". The company had "previously denied any systemic problem with corruption and said the latest Chinese allegations were "deeply concerning to us and contrary to the values of GSK"."

Chapter V - GSK Faces a Bad Day at Black Rock

You know it is going to be a rainy day when your employees line up to testify against your company in an ongoing investigation for bribery and corruption. But those rainy day sighs can move up to a *Bad Day at Black Rock* level when these same employees publicly announce that the company they work for owes them for the creation of fraudulent invoices used by a business unit to fund bribery and corruption which violates not only the FCPA and the UK Bribery Act but also domestic Chinese anti-corruption laws. This happened to GSK when it was announced that certain current employees in its China operation were petitioning the company to reimburse them for bribes they were ordered to pay by their superiors.

In a FT article, it was reported "the UK pharmaceutical company at the centre of a Chinese corruption scandal, is facing protests from junior employees who say the company is refusing to reimburse them for bribes they were ordered to pay by their superiors." While my initial thought was that these Chinese employees had quite a bit of 'cheek' in raising this claim, the more I read into the story, the more I think it may portend serious problems for GSK in any attempt to defend the company going forward. Moreover, "some Chinese sales staff are complaining that GSK has denied bonuses, threatened dismissal or refused to reimburse them for bribes they say were sanctioned by their superiors to boost the company's drug sales. In some cases, managers instructed them to purchase fake receipts that were used to cover up bribes paid in cash or gifts to doctors and hospitals, according to salesmen interviewed by the Financial Times."

The article went on to highlight just how some of these fake invoices, used to gain funds from the corporate headquarters to facilitate bribery and corruption, were generated. "In some instances, managers disguised their involvement by using their personal email address to instruct staff to pay bribes and by ordering junior staff to claim on their personal expense accounts – even if the bribe was actually paid out by the manager – according to these people." Last March, a group of current GSK employees sent a letter to management that said, in part, ""All the expenses were approved by the company". Further, "The expenses were paid with our own money, and although the receipts were not compliant, it was our managers who told us to buy the fake receipts," said one former GSK salesman."

The article quoted that GSK said, "We have zero tolerance for unethical or illegal behaviour and anyone who conducts such behaviour has no place in our company. We believe the vast majority of our employees uphold our values and we welcome employees speaking up if they have concerns." Talk about a 'Speak Up' culture at your company. Probably not exactly what the company had in mind when it invited employees to raise their concerns.

However, as damning as this is, and it would certainly appear to be quite damning, was the following revelation, regarding witness prep during GSK's internal investigation. The article noted, "Some staff were warned not to implicate their supervisors, according to a former salesman: "Our manager approached each person before they were questioned and asked them not to mention his name. He even prepared a story for them to tell the investigator.'""

Dissecting all of the above, it would appear that GSK has several real problems on several fronts. The first is that there appears to have been clear China business unit management participation in the bribery and corruption scheme. While it is still not clear whether the corporate home office was involved in the scheme, simply knew of it or choose to bury its collective head in the sand as to what was going on in China, if your in-country business unit management is involved, it is not too many steps to the corporate home office. Conversely, the question might be that if this fraud against the corporate home office was so open and obvious, why did the corporate office not detect it going forward?

Yet the real issue for the corporate office may be the information about employees being coached to hide evidence during the investigation. If such activity was limited to the 'managers' in the Chinese business units only, what does it say about a corporate office, which allows such witness intimidation? Think that is an investigation *best practice*? However, if the corporate office was involved in any way in such witness intimidation, it will bode extremely poorly in the eyes of the regulators, the UK SFO, which has opened an investigation into the GSK matter and probably the DOJ as well, since GSK is still subject to the CIA it signed back in July of 2012; when it pled guilty and paid *$3 billion* to resolve fraud allegations. Think witness tampering or hiding of evidence might garner the attention of the DOJ for a company already under the equivalent of a Deferred Prosecution Agreement (DPA)?

Chapter VI - GSK's 2001 China Bribery Scandal

It turns out that GSK's 2013/14 bribery and corruption scandal in China was not the company's first brush with such problem, in such a place. An article in the FT by Demetri Sevastopulo and Andrew Ward, entitled "*GSK admits to 2001 Chinese bribery scandal*", reported that GSK had been involved in a prior bribery scandal in China back in 2001, stating, "The Financial Times has learnt that GSK also found problems with its China vaccine business in 2001 that led to the firing of about 30 employees." The article went on to say, "Two people familiar with the 2001 scandal said GSK found that staff were bribing Chinese officials and taking kickbacks. The company acknowledged the matter for the first time to the Financial Times, but said it had dealt with the issue rigorously."

Obviously having a prior bribery scandal in the very same country as another current scandal portends poorly for GSK, "The US Department of Justice, which is investigating the current allegations, will take a close look at the earlier scandal, said a former senior DoJ official who asked to remain anonymous. If it found a pattern of such behaviour, the justice department was likely to take a tougher stance towards the company, legal experts said." The FT article quoted Timothy Blakely, a partner at the US law firm of Morrison & Foerster, who said, "US prosecutors would have to examine the 2001 case under justice department guidelines to see whether there was a pattern of behaviour. "It is something that a prosecutor would have to take into account.""

Unfortunately for GSK the 2001 scandal has some other rather inconvenient facts, which may well impact how the company fares in the current imbroglio in which it finds itself. The first fact is that unlike the current scandal, which unfolded beginning in 2013 when an anonymous whistleblower presented evidence of bribery and corruption in the company's China operations, in the 2001 scandal the company took swift actions to investigate the allegations. In 2001, GSK hired PricewaterhouseCoopers (PwC) to investigate the allegations "at the time the corruption suspicions emerged." The 2001 investigation, as noted above, led to the termination of "about 30 (GSK) employees".

One of the difficulties for GSK is this robust response in 2001 contrasts dramatically with its response in 2013. It is now known that GSK was notified by the anonymous whistleblower of allegations of bribery and corruption as early as January 2013. Yet the company gave itself a clean bill of health, finding no evidence of any wrongdoing. However, it did not take Chinese authorities long at all to investigate and conclude that there was "evidence of "massive and systemic bribery"" in GSK's China business operations.

Interestingly, one of the PwC investigators back in 2001 has played prominently in circumstances around this current bribery scandal. That person is Peter Humphrey who was indicted for his actions around some of GSK's current bribery and corruption issues. The FT reported that "One member of the PwC team in 2001 was Peter Humphrey. Now an independent investigator, he is being held in China on charges of illegally buying private information in connection with GSK's current scandal." If he was part of the investigation team back in 2001, do you think he might have inquired about any current allegations of bribery or corruption or any ongoing company investigations? What are the implications for GSK if he did make such inquiries but was not given correct information? Does he have a claim back against GSK?

Another very interesting issue for GSK is that its current Chief Executive Officer (CEO), Sir Andrew Witty, "was the company's head of Asia-Pacific, but his responsibilities excluded China. GSK said Sir Andrew "was not involved in and was not aware of" the 2001 Chinese bribery case at the time. Sir Andrew has tried to cast GSK as a leader in ethical reforms since it was hit with a record $3bn DoJ fine for marketing abuses in 2012. But his clean-up effort, including measures to cut the link between sales volume and pay for marketing personnel, has been overshadowed by the latest scandal in China."

All of these 'coincidences' may lead the DOJ or the UK SFO to conclude that GSK has a culture of non-compliance or worse yet - a culture of corruption. The FT article cited to un-named legal experts for the following, "If prosecutors find a pattern of such behavior, they are likely to take a tougher stance towards the company." Do not forget that GSK had paid a $3bn fine for false marketing and is currently under a CIA, the equivalent of a DPA, for those illegal actions.

Chapter VII - No Sex Please, We're British: The Sex Tape

I thought about that ubiquitous work of British visual and audio entertainment, *No Sex Please, We're British*, when the revelations from late June 2014 that the GSK corruption scandal all started with a sex tape. In an article in the MailOnline, entitled "*How a secret sex tape plunged British drugs giant Glaxo in a £90million bribery probe*", Rebecca Evans reported "A covert sex tape involving a senior executive and his Chinese lover was the trigger for a major investigation into corruption at British drugs giant GlaxoSmith-Kline, it was revealed yesterday. The video of married Mark Reilly and his girlfriend was filmed by secret camera and emailed anonymously to board members of the pharmaceutical firm. It led to an investigation that has rocked the £76billion company – which stands accused of bribing doctors and other health officials in China with £320million of gifts, including sexual favours from prostitutes, to persuade them to prescribe its drugs."

This sex tape, along with allegations of bribery and corruption, were sent to GSK Board members, including CEO Sir Andrew Witty, in March 2013 by someone with the brilliantly named email address, "*GSK Whistleblower*". Evans reported that two additional emails "making serious fraud allegations" were sent as well, one in January and one in May. In an article in the WSJ, entitled "*Sex Video Sheds Light in Glaxo China Case*", Laurie Burkitt reported that "The British drug maker regarded the video—apparently shot without the executive's knowledge—as a breach of security, the person said." Evans reported that in addition to this security breach, GSK believed the sex tape to be a "threat or blackmail attempt".

One of GSK's responses was to hire the firm ChinaWhys Co., to investigate the matter. The firm's principals, former fraud investigator Peter Humphrey and Yu Yingzeng, a naturalized US citizen, were not able to determine who placed the video camera in Reilly's Shanghai apartment, who shot the video or who sent it to GSK executives. However Evans reported "But a few months after starting to investigate Miss Shi, Mr Humphrey was arrested along with his wife Yu Yingzeng, a US citizen and daughter of one of China's most eminent atomic weapons scientists. According to the Sunday Times, Mr Humphrey's arrest and detention in July was at around the same time that China began a police probe into GSK's alleged bribery." And, unfortunately for Humphrey and his wife, they were arrested last August for allegedly breaking of Chinese laws relating to information privacy.

In addition to the investigation into the provenance of the sex tape and its sender, GSK had also engaged in an internal investigation into the substantive allegations of bribery brought forward by the "*GSK Whistleblower*" in emails to the GSK Board in January and May, 2013. As reported by Evans, "The emails laid out a series of sales and marketing practices described as 'pervasive corruption'." Unfortunately for the company, GSK "found 'no specific evidence' to substantiate the claims. However, the accusations are virtually identical to the charges laid by police against

Mr Reilly and 45 other suspects. Last month, Britain's SFO announced it is to investigate the company's 'commercial practices'."

'Honey-pots' and 'Sparrow-nests' are well known terms for anyone who has read cold war tales of espionage between the former Soviet Union and the US. However, the Reilly sex-tape and the GSK bribery scandal would seem to be an entirely different can of worms. In an article in Time, entitled *"What the GSK Sex Tape Says About Surveillance in China"*, Hannah Beech wrote that in China, "Surveillance - or the threat of surveillance — is a constant in China. As a journalist, I may be more interesting to the powers that be than some other foreigners here. But other expat friends who've been followed, hacked or otherwise tracked in China include diplomats, NGO staff and businesspeople. Also, artists and academics." Such surveillance includes having "email auto-forwarding mysteriously activated or to be tailed by a black Audi while on assignment in the Chinese countryside."

It does seem incredible that any serious internal investigation could fail to turn up any of the evidence that the Chinese government has been able to develop against GSK. This points to the absolute importance of your internal investigations. Although the GSK investigation was focused in China, the same is true in the US, particularly for a US listed company subject to Dodd-Frank. Further, we must invoke that well-known British author George Orwell for reminding you that in some countries Big Brother really is watching you. And finally, you may not be paranoid as people really may be watching you and filming your most intimate acts.

Chapter VIII - Things Only Get Worse for GSK

Christopher M. Matthews and Hester Plumridge writing in a WSJ article entitled *"FBI, SEC Start Glaxo Inquiries Over China"*, reported that in late July 2014 "Glaxo received an anonymous email claiming its employees in Syria bribed doctors and pharmacists over the past five years to promote products including painkiller Panadol and toothpaste Sensodyne. The bribes took the form of cash payments, speaking fees, trips, free dinners and free samples, said the email, which was reviewed by The Wall Street Journal. The email cited names and dates. Syrian health officials allegedly received bribes from Glaxo employees to fast-track registration of its Sensodyne dental products, including cash payments and a trip to a 2011 conference in Rome, the email maintains. Glaxo employees also were involved in smuggling a narcotic product from Syria into Iran, the email alleges. The product in question, pseudoephedrine, is a raw ingredient of Glaxo's congestion medicine Actifed."

GSK once again reiterated its previously announced position that it was firmly against the payments of bribes by its employees. In response to the allegations of bribes paid in Syria the WSJ article said, "Glaxo said it would thoroughly investigate all claims made in the Syria email, and said it has asked the sender for more information. The company said it has zero tolerance for unethical behavior, adding, "We welcome people speaking up if they have concerns about alleged misconduct.""

Much more problematic for GSK is the fact that both the SEC and DOJ opened formal investigations into allegations of bribery and corruption by the company. The WSJ piece notes, "Federal Bureau of Investigation agents have been interviewing current and former GlaxoSmithKline employees in connection with bribery allegations in China, according to a person familiar with the matter, as fresh claims of corruption surfaced against Glaxo's operations in Syria. The interviews have taken place in Washington, D.C., in the past few months and are part of a Justice Department investigation into Glaxo's activities in China, the person added. The U.S. Securities and Exchange Commission also is investigating the company's business in China, according to people familiar with the matter." This is for a company that pled guilty to the US Government for fraud in marketing, paid a $3bn fine only a few years ago, entered into a CIA and promised never to do it again.

GSK now finds itself under investigation, either internally or by anti-corruption regulators across the globe in at least four countries. Unlike other companies that have found systemic issues of bribery and corruption or systemic failures in internal controls, the allegations of bribery and corruption are not 10-15 years old.

Chapter IX - International Ripples From the Chinese Corruption Investigations

The effects of the GSK bribery scandal expanded far beyond the geographic limits of China. In an article in the FT, entitled *"Beijing probe touches west's cereal bowls"*, Lucy Hornby wrote about some of the ripple effects of the GSK corruption investigation. Her basic thesis was set out in the first line of her piece, "Never before have China's domestic politics had such ramifications for global business." She wrote about two tangible examples of what she termed the "ripple effects" of the Chinese anti-corruption investigation, which began in earnest last summer with the revelations of corruption by GSK.

Hornby reported that the stock price for a Canadian company, Athabasca Oil Corporation, "the partner company for major Chinese investments in Canadian oil sands – fell 13 per cent this week. It is down 24 per cent since the beginning of April, when Athabasca announced PetroChina, a listed unit of CNPC, would buy the 40 per cent of the Dover oil sands project that it did not already own. Since then, two executives from PetroChina's Canadian operations have fallen prey to the corruption purge – and the C$1.32bn (US$1.23bn) transfer payment has not been made." But these ripples have also reached the British breakfast table as Chinese authorities announced they were investigating the owner of the company that makes the breakfast staple Weetabix.

Business ventures in other countries such as Cambodia and Australia have been put off due to the Chinese corruption investigation. This has been because of both corrupt payments made to Chinese officials and, in some cases, corrupt payments alleged to have been made by Chinese officials. For instance in Cambodia a project that was mired in such problems that the primary funding partner, The World Bank, had suspended funding has now run into such problems that Standard Chartered may lose up to $250MM in funding which it provided. Further, Hornby reported that "In Australia last year, a A$1.4bn bid for Sundance Resources – which had proposed a $A5bn iron ore mine on the border of Cameroon and the Republic of Congo – collapsed after high-flying Chinese entrepreneur Liu Han abruptly vanished. Mr Liu had built his mining business by cultivating ties with Mr Zhou while the latter governed southwestern Sichuan province. He was sentenced to death in May for organised crime. His defence was that he was carrying out orders for unnamed "leaders"."

Things are particularly difficult at PetroChina, a major investor in Canadian oil sands, because, as Hornby noted, "dozens of senior executives have been detained or questioned in the past year. Many, including the head of its Indonesian business, played key roles in its international projects." However Hornby believes that "capital expenditure commitments by state-owned enterprises are likely to be honoured as the investigation continues, because China's large and growing economy has a fundamental need for resources."

Another large Chinese energy concern CNPC has also been hard hit by the corruption scandal. Attached, as a diagram, to Hornby's article is a graphic that shows the extent of the company's investments of the past 10 years or so. The graphic also notes that the company "has been hardest hit by the ongoing corruption purge, with dozens of senior executives detained or questioned." The chart below shows the "ripple effects" of CNPC investment.

Country	Investment Amount
Kazakhstan	$12.7bn
Peru	$2.6bn
Turkmenistan	$1.2bn
Scotland	$1bn
Ecuador	$0.7bn
Australia	$4.1bn
Canada	$3.3bn
Syria	$0.6bn
Mozambique	$4.2bn

Hornby's article touched on another area, which has significance for the FCPA practitioner, that begs the question of whether a state-owned enterprise is an instrumentality or in any other way covered by the FCPA? She wrote that "the unusually public nature of this corruption investigation has given outsiders a clearer insight into the way money and power have become entwined, and influence dealmaking, in today's China." She quoted Luke Patey, author of the book *The New Kings of Crude*, for the following, ""For years, Chinese national oil companies have fought hard against the label that they are political instruments of the Chinese government and Communist party. That political nature is now on full display.""

Hornby's article demonstrates not only the pervasive nature of Chinese corruption but also how many countries such corruption may have effected. It also dispels those FCPA naysayers who argue that the law brings a competitive disadvantage to US companies. Many of these Chinese investments are now on hold with no hope of completion or even funding because of the domestic turmoil inside China over corruption. Companies and countries want a reliable business partner, starting with one which does not engage in bribery and corruption to obtain a contract and then onto a company which fulfills its contractual obligations. Think about that as a selling point the next time you are oversees.

Chapter X - Missed Red Flags

One of the questions that GSK must answer for US and UK regulators is how such a massive bribery and corruption scheme occurred in its Chinese operations? It is not as if the Chinese market was not well known for its propensity towards corruption, well over 20% of recent FCPA enforcement actions related to companies violating the law in their Chinese operations.

A. Types of Bribery Schemes

The types of bribery schemes in China are also well known. In a FT article, entitled "*Bribery built into the fabric of Chinese healthcare system*", reporters Jamil Anderlini and Tom Mitchell wrote about the 'nuts and bolts' of how bribery occurs in the health care industry in China. They opened their article by noting that the practice of bribing "doctors, hospital administrators and health officials is rampant." They quoted an un-named senior health official in Beijing for the following, "All foreign and domestic pharmaceuticals operating in China are equally corrupt". The authors also quoted Shaun Rein, a Shanghai-based consultant and author of "*The End of Cheap China*", for the following "This is a systemic problem and foreign pharmaceutical companies are in a conundrum. If they want to grow in China they have to give bribes. It's not a choice because officials in health ministry, hospital administrators and doctors demand it."

Their article included a diagram which visually represented two methods used to pay bribes in China, which were designated the *direct incentives* and *indirect incentives* methods. Whichever method is used, the goal is the same – to boost sales.

In the *direct incentives* method, a third party representative of a company would provide cash to the department head of a clinic or hospital. The department head would in turn pay it to the individual physicians to encourage them to prescribe the company's medical products. But a third party representative could also contact a physician directly and reward them with "gifts such as storecards, vouchers and travel" expenses. Other *direct* methods might include the opening of bank accounts or charge accounts at luxury goods store and then the company would hand "the debit card or VIP card directly to the recipient."

The FT noted that the *indirect incentives* method tended to be "used by larger pharmaceutical groups with stricter governance procedures." Under this bribery scheme there were two recognized manners to get benefits into the hands of prescribing physicians. The first is to have cash incentives paid to a third party representative, such as a travel agency, which would then "pass on some of these rewards to the physician directly." Another method was for the company itself to make a "lump sum sponsorship paid to hospitals". The hospitals would then distribute perks "to the doctors as a monthly or annual bonus." Another *indirect* method noted was that companies might organize overseas conferences and site visits, which might also include first class travel arrangements with stays at "five-star accommodations."

Anderlini and Mitchell reported that "The 2012 annual reports of half a dozen listed Chinese pharmaceutical companies reveal the companies paid out enormous sums in "sales expenses", including travel costs and fees for sales meetings, marketing "business development" and "other expenses". Most of the largest expenses were "travel costs or meeting fees and the expenses of the companies' sales teams were, in every case, several multiples of the net profits each company earned last year." They cited the example of the company Guizhou Yibai Pharmaceutical which earned a net profit last year of Rmb333.3m. However its "sales expenses came to a total of Rmb1.25bn, including meetings expenses of more than Rmb295m and wages of just Rmb88m." Indeed the "largest expense for the company's sales team of 2,318 people was Rmb404m spent on travel, for an average of more than Rmb174,000 per sales representative for the year. That is roughly what it would cost every single sales representative to fly 10 times a month between Beijing and Guiyang, where the company is based."

B. Auditing Responses - Missed Red Flags?

But what should GSK have done if such expense were kept 'off the books'? Ben Hirschler in a Reuters article, entitled "How GlaxoSmithKline misses red flags in China", quoted one un-named source for the following, ""You'd look at invoices and expenses, and it would all look legitimate," said a senior executive at one top accountancy firm." The problem with fraud - if it is good fraud - is it is well hidden, and when there is collusion high up then it is very difficult to detect."" Jeremy Gordon, director of China Business Services, was quoted that "There is a disconnect between the global decision makers and the guys running things on the ground. It's about initially identifying red flags and then searching for specifics."

There are legitimate reasons to hold Continuing Medical Conferences (CME), such as to make physicians aware of products and the latest advances in medicine. However, this legitimate purpose can easily be corrupted. Hirschler quoted Paul Gillis, author of the China Accounting Blog, for the following "Travel agencies are used like ATMs in China to distribute out illegal payments. Any company that does not have their internal audit department all over travel agency spending is negligent." Based on this, GSK should have looked more closely on marketing expenses and more particularly, the monies spent on travel agencies. Hirschler wrote, "They [un-named auditing experts] say that one red flag was the number of checks being written to travel agencies for sending doctors to medical conferences, although this may have been blurred by the fact that CME accounts for a huge part of drug industry marketing."

One other issue might be materiality. If GSK's internal auditors had not been trained that there is no materiality standard under the FCPA, they may have missed a large number of payments made that were under a company's governance procedure for elevated review of expenses. Further, if more than one auditor was involved with more than one travel agency, they may not have been able to connect the dots regarding the totality of payments made to one travel agency.

What about the external auditors, PwC? Francine McKenna, who writes and speaks extensively on all things related to Big 4 auditing, wrote last year, in blog post entitled *"What The SEC And PCAOB Fail To Acknowledge About Chinese Fraud"*, that Pam Chepiga of Allen & Overy, "told the audience that FCPA investigations in China are difficult because, "you can't take the documents out of the country."" After her panel, Chepiga told McKenna "that not only does China restrict the dissemination of documents outside of China, but internal investigations by multinationals must be done by Chinese lawyers with support from the Chinese accounting firms." Given the experience that the SEC is having with Deloitte, it seems, "previous cooperation agreements are not in force. The SEC would have a hard time going over and investigating a fraud or FCPA violation by the Chinese arm of a US based company". So things may not have been any easier for PwC as well. However the recent agreement between the SEC and the Chinese Securities Regulatory Commission will allows the SEC some access to audit the work papers of Chinese companies listed in the US may influence this question.

C. Ongoing Monitoring

Another response that GSK could have implemented was to engage in greater ongoing monitoring. An article in the Texas Lawyer, Out of Order column, entitled *"5 Tips for Avoiding Email Compliance Traps"*, by Alexandra Wrage, President of TRACE International, cited back to a WSJ article, entitled *"Glaxo Probes Tactics Used to Market Botox in China"*, which reported that internal Glaxo documents and emails reviewed by the Wall Street Journal show Glaxo's China sales staff was apparently instructed by local managers to use their personal email addresses to discuss marketing strategies related to Botox. In the personal emails, sales staff discuss rewarding doctors for prescribing Botox with cash payments, credits that could be used to meet medical education requirements and other rewards."

With the technology available to companies today it is possible that companies have the ability to determine if employees are accessing personal email accounts from business computers. Wrage used the GSK matter as a jumping off point "For companies wanting to get a handle on the compliance risks they face through email (mis)uses and other forms of technology". She gives five tips. (1) Encourage communication between compliance and IT departments. (2) Map out your universe of data. (3) Know your obligations, then develop an established set of policies and procedures around them. (4) Train employees to speak up about the new uses in technology. (5) Stress-test your program.

Chapter XI - The Problem of Fake Invoices in China

In an article in the NYT, entitled *"Coin of Realm in China Graft: Phony Receipts"*, reporter David Barboza wrote about the buying and selling of business and tax receipts on the black market in China. Barboza said that "To begin to comprehend China's vast underground economy, one need only visit this city's major transportation depots and watch as peddlers openly hawk fake receipts. A scalper mumbles, "Fapiao, fapiao," or 'Receipts' at the Shanghai Railway Station. The trade in receipts is more or less open. A woman in her 30s called out to passers-by as her two children play near the city's south train station, "We sell all types of receipts." While many buyers use them to defraud employers and evade taxes, they have recently come under FCPA and UK Bribery Act scrutiny due to the ongoing investigation of GSK which apparently is "still trying to figure out how four senior executives at its China operation were able to submit fake receipts to embezzle millions of dollars over the last six years. Police officials say that some of the cash was used to create a slush fund to bribe doctors, hospitals and government officials."

In many cases it is not the paper that the receipts are printed on that is fake, only the information contained therein which is fraudulent. For instance, the unused receipts from a hotel may be pilfered and "then resold to dealers and enter the black market. In Shanghai, companies actually advertise by fax that they buy unused receipts. One such advertisement sent by fax read "Due to our diverse accounting service for other companies, we now need invoices from various industries (13% or 17% VAT)." Another ad sent by the Shanghai Fangyuan Accounting Agency reads, referring to the value-added tax receipts, "If your company has leftovers of 13% or 17% VAT invoices, we can offer good rates to buy them."

Using an older form of advertising, Barboza noted that, "Signs posted throughout this city advertise all kinds of fake receipts: travel receipts, lease receipts, waste material receipts and value-added tax receipts. Promotions for counterfeit "fapiao" (the Chinese word for an official invoice) are sent by fax and through mobile phone text messages. On China's popular e-commerce Web site, Taobao.com, sellers even promise special discounts and same-day delivery of forged receipts."

As bad as this system of selling fraudulent invoices is, it pales beside the danger created by the sale of invoices by government officials themselves. Barboza wrote that "state employees, whether they work for government agencies or state-owned enterprises, seem as eager as anyone else to bolster their compensation by filing fake invoices." He quoted Wang Yuhua, an assistant professor of political science at the University of Pennsylvania and the author of a study on bribery and corruption in China, for the following "Their salaries are relatively low, so they supplement a lot of it with reimbursements. This is hard to monitor."

Barboza reported that "In the Glaxo case, Chinese investigators say the drugmaker's top Chinese executives worked closely in recent years with a Shanghai travel agency to falsify documents. For instance, airline ticket receipts were filed for trips that never took place and when executives listed 100 guests at a conference, perhaps only 80 showed up, making it possible to file false inflated receipts and thus embezzle from Glaxo's London headquarters." Six other international pharmaceutical companies have also acknowledged that they have used this travel agency in the past three years.

Barboza detailed that such corruption schemes were not unknown to FCPA enforcement. He cited to the SEC complaints against IBM where its "employees in China created "slush funds" with its travel agencies and business partners, partly to "provide cash payments and imported gifts, such as cameras and laptop computers to Chinese government officials."" In another SEC Complaint, it found that "between 2005 and 2010, Wyeth, a division of the drug company Pfizer, had "submitted false or inflated invoices for organizing large-scale consumer education events.""

The FCPA Blog reported, in a post entitled "*Baxter confirms China payment offenses*", that the company in question paid for an event which never occurred. It paid a travel agency identified as the Beijing Youth Travel Service Co. approximately $15,100 for a conference at the Crowne Plaza Shenyang Parkview. The article quoted the WSJ which had written, "But an employee in the banquet and meeting department of the Crowne Plaza Shenyang Parkview said no event was organized for that date involving Baxter or medicines. She also said the hotel had no record of a meeting on that date organized by the Beijing Youth Travel Agency."

Barboza refers to some un-named analysts who "say the cost of monitoring is high and would involve the tedious work of verifying millions of receipts by calling hotels, airlines and office supply stores and scrutinizing countless transactions for signs of fraud." My response to these analysts is to say that if your compliance risks are known for a certain profile, then you should devote the necessary resources to making sure you are in compliance in that area. Eric Carlson pointed out in his three post series in the FCPA Blog, entitled "*Corruption Risk—China Travel Edition*", that there have been a plethora of FCPA enforcement actions related to travel in China. With regard to the abuse through travel agencies, Carlson wrote about four different corruption scenarios, including (1) event abuse planning, (2) mixture of legitimate and illegitimate travel; (3) other collusion with travel agencies; and (4) parallel itineraries. So those risks are well known and have been documented.

II. The Convictions

Chapter XII - Humphrey and Wife Convicted

When it was announced in July, 2014 that Peter William Humphrey, a 58-year-old British national, and his wife, Yu Yingzeng, a 61-year-old American, would go on trial on charges of illegally purchasing personal information about Chinese nationals in Shanghai's No. 1 Intermediate People's Court, the trial was originally scheduled to be closed to the public. However later in July, Chinese officials announced that the trial would be 'open' although the degree of openness is not completely clear.

Further the couple's son, Harvey Humphrey, was allowed visited his parents in their detention center in Pudong, Shanghai, for the first time since their arrest. The visit came after some fierce lobbying by the US and UK consulates. As reported in the online publication FiercePharma, in an article entitled "*GSK private eyes' son allowed first visit to parents in China jail as trial nears*", their son said, "They didn't quite believe I was coming. They were quite overwhelmed. My mum was shocked. My dad held himself together," the younger Humphrey told the paper. "It's a bit unusual for the Chinese to do this. I feel something has changed in the Chinese approach to my parents." Son Harvey had written to the GSK's CEO Sir Andrew Witty last December to "take a few minutes to raise my father's case" during a visit to the country, he told the FT, "I understand everything is complicated in China but it seems my parents are paying a big price".

In that one-day trial Peter Humphrey and his wife Ms. Yu, were convicted of illegally purchasing information on Chinese citizens. In a FT article, entitled "*China court hands GSK investigator jail term and orders deportation*", Gabriel Wildau and Andrew Ward reported that husband Humphrey received a two and a half year jail term which was "just short of the three-year maximum". In an article in the WSJ, entitled "*China Convicts Two Corporate Investigators*", James T. Areddy and Laurie Burkitt reported that he was also ordered to pay a fine of approximately $32,500 and will be deported from the country when his jail term is completed. Ms. Yu received a two year jail term and was ordered to pay a fine of approximately $23,000 but will be allowed to remain in the country after her sentence is completed. Both announced after the trial that they would not appeal their sentences.

In a NYT article, entitled "*In China, British Investigator Hired by Glaxo, and Wife, Sentenced to Prison*", David Barboza reported that the couple "acknowledged that from 2009 to 2013, they obtained about 250 pieces of private information about individuals, including government-issued identity documents, entry and exit travel records and mobile phone records, all apparently in violation of China's privacy laws." According to the NYT article, Ms. Yu claimed that she did not know her actions where illegal and was quoted as saying, "We did not know obtaining these pieces of information was illegal in China. If I had known I would have destroyed the evidence." According to the WSJ, the privacy law which was the basis of the conviction, was enacted in

2009 "to make it illegal to handle certain personal medical records and telephone records" but that the law itself "remains vague" on what precisely might constitute violation.

From the court statements, however, it did appear that the couple had trafficked in personal information. As reported by the WSJ, "In separate responses over more than 10 hours, Mr. Humphreys and Ms. Yu denied that their firm trafficked in personal information, saying they had hired others to obtain personal data when clients requested it." From the documents presented by the prosecution, it would seem clear that the couple had obtained items which were more personal in nature. They were alleged by prosecutors to have "used hidden cameras to gather information as well as government records on identification numbers, family members, real-estate holdings, vehicle owner, telephone logs and travel records."

Recognizing the verdicts under Chinese law are usually predetermined and the trials are scripted affairs, there is, nonetheless, important information communicated to the outside world by this trial. First and foremost is, as reported in the NYT article is a "chilling effect on companies that engage in due diligence work for global companies, many of whom believe the couple may have been unfairly targeted." The WSJ article went further quoting Geoffrey Sant for the following, "It impacts all attempts to do business between the U.S. and China because it will be very challenging to verify the accuracy of company or personal financial information." In other words, things just got a lot tougher to perform, what most companies would expect to be a minimum level of due diligence.

Second is the time frame noted in the court statements as to the time of the violations, from 2009 to 2013. Many had assumed that Humphrey and Yu's arrests related to their investigation work on behalf of the GSK, which was trying to determine who had filmed a sex tape of the company's head of Chinese operations, which was then provided to the company via an anonymous whistleblower. This would seem to beg the question of whether the couple would have been prosecuted if they had not engaged in or accepted the GSK assignment.

Chapter XIII - GSK Convicted

"GSK plc sincerely apologies to the Chinese patients,
doctors and hospitals, and the Chinese Government and the
Chinese people."

With those words, GSK was convicted in a secret trial in September 2014, in a court in the Hunan province of China for bribery and corruption related to its Chinese business unit. The amount of the fine was approximately $491MM. This fine was the largest levied on a western company for bribery and corruption in China. Moreover, if it had been in the US for a violation of the FCPA, it would have come in as the third highest fine of all-time, behind those of Siemens and Halliburton. In a FT article, entitled *"GSK hit with record $490m China fine for bribing doctors"*, reporters Andrew Ward and Patti Waldmeir noted that the fine is "equal to the Rmb 3bn in bribes that Chinese investigators said had been paid by GSK."

While it is not entirely clear when the trial was held or how long the trial lasted, it appeared that it was in the same range as the one-day trial given to Peter Humphrey and his wife last month, when they were both found guilty for violating China's privacy laws. In an article in the NYT, entitled *"Glaxo Fined $500 Million By China"*, Keith Bradsher and Chris Buckley reported, "Chinese authorities accused Glaxo of bribing hospitals and doctors, channeling illicit kickbacks through travel agencies and pharmaceutical industry associations — a scheme that brought the company higher drug prices and illegal revenue of more than $150 million. In a rare move, authorities also prosecuted the foreign-born executive who ran Glaxo's Chinese unit." Moreover, GSK China's country manager, Mark Reilly and four other in-country executives were each convicted with potential sentences of up to four years in prison. The NYT noted, "the sentences were suspended, allowing the defendants to avoid incarceration if they stay out of trouble, according to Xinhua. The verdict indicated that Mr. Reilly could be promptly deported. The report said they had pleaded guilty and would not appeal."

A WSJ article, entitled *"Meet the Glaxo Executives Convicted in China"*, detailed the five GSK executives' crimes and sentences, the summary is as follows:

- Mark Reilly: GSK's former China chief. He was sentenced to prison for three years with a four-year suspension. He was also the victim of an illicit recording of he and his girlfriend with the sex tape delivered to GSK management in London.
- Zhang Guowei: GSK China's former HR Director, who was sentenced to three years in prison with a three-year suspension. Chinese state media said he admitted that the company has used many bribery schemes to ensure the sales of high price drugs to Chinese consumers.
- Liang Hong: Former GSK China's vice president and operations manager. He was sentenced to two years in prison with a three-year suspension. On Chinese state-

controlled television he said he gave bribes to government officials, hospital administrators and doctors via travel agencies to pave the way for drug sales.

- Zhao Hongyan: GSK China's former legal-affairs director. Ms. Zhao was sentenced to two years in prison with a two-year suspension. On state-controlled television Ms. Zhao said she destroyed evidence relating to bribery to avoid punishment.
- Huang Hong: Huang was a GSK China's business-development manager. She was sentenced three years in prison with a four-year suspension. The WSJ article reported that she was accused of giving and taking bribes; and informed Chinese officials that GSK China used funds labeled for public relations use to maintain relationships with "major clients," who she said were hospital administrators.

The suspension of the sentences was highly significant. The FT article quoted from the trial court that the sentences had resulted directly because "they confessed the facts truthfully and were considered to have given themselves up." The WSJ article reported that the court also took into account that GSK China country manager Reilly had "voluntarily returned to China, assisted in the investigation and confessed…and had "truthfully recounted the crimes of his employer."" Also they were in stark contrast to the three-year and two-year sentences handed down to Humphrey and his wife respectively last month. There was no word from GSK, however, on whether it would terminate some or all of the convicted executives.

GSK itself made several interesting statements about the bribery allegations and conclusions of the trial court. The FT article quoted CEO Sir Andrew Witty, for the following, "Reaching a conclusion in the investigation of our Chinese Business is important, but this has been a deeply disappointing matter for GSK. We have and will continue to learn from this. GSK has been in China for close to a hundred years, and we remain fully committed to the country and its people." The company went further in statements. In addition to the quote above, GSK was quoted in the NYT article as saying, "that it "fully accepts the facts and evidence of the investigation, and the verdict of the Chinese judicial authorities."" The FT article added further clarification when it said that GSK " had "co-operated fully with the authorities and has taken steps to comprehensively rectify the issues identified at the operations of GSK China.""

These statements of contrition are quite a distance from the place where GSK started last summer when the bribery allegations broke when the company tried to use the 'rogue employee(s)' defense, when it said that the bribery and corruption involved only a "few rogue Chinese-born employees" that were "outside our systems of controls" *Oops*.

The NYT reported that GSK also said, "that the court, the Changsha Intermediate People's Court, had found the company guilty only of bribing nongovernmental personnel." This is significant because the bribery of a government official (defined as such in China and not under the FCPA) is a much more serious crime in China. The British Embassy in China also weighed in, at least slightly, with the following statement, "We note the verdict in this case. We have continually called for a just conclusion in the case in accordance with Chinese law. It would be wrong to comment while the case remains open to appeal."

Chapter XIV - Some Thoughts on the Verdict

Did GSK obtain a negotiated settlement with the Chinese government when it was announced that the company pled guilty to bribery and corruption and was fined almost $500MM by a Chinese court? Further, what lessons can be drawn from the GSK matter for companies operating in China and the compliance practitioner going forward?

I think the first lesson to draw is that the Chinese government will focus more on companies than on individuals. Andrew Ward, Patti Waldmeir and Caroline Binham, writing in a FT article, entitled *"Pain from graft scandal likely to linger"*, quoted Mak Yuen Teen, a corporate governance expert at the National University of Singapore, for the following, "By handing suspended sentences rather than jail terms to Mark Reilly, GSK's former head of China, and four of his top lieutenants, the court in Hunan province was holding the company more accountable than the individuals."

However other commentators said, "GSK got off more lightly than expected for bribing doctors to prescribe its drugs." The article went on to note, "People close to the situation denied that the outcome amounted to a negotiated settlement. But Bing Shaowen, a Chinese pharmaceuticals analyst, said it was likely that GSK made commitments on research and development investment and drug pricing to avoid more draconian treatment. A further FT article by Ward, Waldmeir and Binham, entitled *"GSK closes a chapter with £300m fine but story likely to run on"*, cited Dan Roules, an anti-corruption expert at the Shanghai firm Squire Sanders, who said that he had expected the penalty to be harsher. Roules was quoted as saying "The fact that GSK co-operated with the authorities would have made a difference." The article went on to say that Roules "pointed to GSK's statement on Friday pledging to become "a model for reform in China's healthcare industry" by "supporting China's scientific development" and increasing access to its products "through pricing flexibility"."

What about reputational damage leading to a drop in the value of stock? The market had an interesting take on the GSK conviction, it yawned. Moreover, as noted in the FT Lex Column "The stock market was never bothered. The shares moved little when the investigation, and then the fine, were disclosed." Why did the market have such a reaction? The Lex Column said that one of the reasons might be that "China may be too small to matter much for now" to the company.

Another lesson is one that Matt Kelly, editor of Compliance Week, wrote about in the context of the National Football League's (NFL) Ray Rice scandal, in an article entitled *"The NFL's True Problem: Misplaced Priorities Trumping Ethics & Compliance"*, when he said that a company must align its "core values with its core priorities." GSK moved towards doing that throughout the last year, during the investigation into the bribery and corruption scandal in China. Although CEO, Sir Andrew Witty, has been a champion for ethical reform in both the company and greater pharmaceutical industry, the FT reporters noted that the China corruption scandal, coupled with "smaller-scale corruption allegations in the Middle East and Poland, has raised fresh questions about ethical standards and compliance." If Witty wants to move GSK forward, he must strive to align the company's business priorities with his (and the company's) stated ethical values.

Which brings us to some of the successes that GSK has created in the wake of the bribery and corruption scandal. These successes are instructive because they present concrete steps that the compliance practitioner can take to help facilitate such change. As reported by Katie Thomas, in a NYT article entitled "*Glaxo to Stop Paying Doctors To Boost Drugs*", one change that GSK has instituted is that it will no longer pay doctors to promote its products and will stop tying compensation of sales representatives to the number of prescriptions doctors write, which were two common pharmaceutical sales practices that have been criticized as troublesome conflicts of interest. While this practice has gone on for many, many years it had been prohibited in the US through a pharmaceutical industry-imposed ethics code but is still used in other countries outside the US.

In addition to this ban on paying doctors to speak favorably about its products at conferences, GSK will also change its compensation structure so that it will no longer compensate sales representatives based on the number of prescriptions that physicians write, a standard practice that some have said pushed pharmaceutical sales officials to inappropriately promote drugs to doctors. Now GSK pays its sales representatives based on their technical knowledge, the quality of service they provided to clients to improve patient care, and the company's business performance.

In addition to the obvious conflict of interest, which apparently is an industry wide conflict of interest because multiple companies have engaged in these tactics, there is also clearly the opportunity for abuse leading to allegations of illegal bribery and corruption. Indeed one of the key bribery schemes alleged to have been used by GSK in China was to pay doctors, hospital administrators and other government officials, bonuses based upon the amount of GSK pharmaceutical products, which they may have prescribed to patients. But with this new program in place, perhaps GSK may have "removed the incentive to do anything inappropriate."

This new compensation and marketing program by GSK demonstrates that companies can make substantive changes in compensation, which promote not only better compliance but also promote better business relationships. A company spokesman interviewed in the NYT piece noted that the changes GSK will make abroad had already been made in the US and because of these changes, "the experience in the United States had been positive and had improved relationships with doctors and medical institutions."

In addition to these changes in compensation and marketing, Ward, Waldmeir and Binham reported that GSK announced it would strive to be "a model for reform in China's healthcare industry" by "supporting China's scientific development" and increasing access to its products "through pricing flexibility". They further stated "Rival companies will now be watching nervously to see whether more enforcement action takes place in a sector where inducements for prescribing drugs have long been an important source of income for poorly paid Chinese medics," which is probably not going to be a return to the wild west of bribery and corruption that occurred over the past few years in China. Shaowen was quoted as saying that the GSK matter "is a very historic case for the Chinese pharmaceutical industry. It means that strict compliance will become the routine and the previous drug marketing and sales methods must be abolished." But the company still faces real work to rebuild its reputation in China. Moreover, it still faces legal scrutiny for its conduct in the UK under the Bribery Act and the US under the FCPA.

III. What Does It All Mean?

Chapter XV - What Can You Do?

If your company has Chinese operations, what should you do? Christopher M. Matthews, in a WSJ article entitled "*Western Companies Sweat as Glaxo Probe Unfolds*", warned that "The rapidly unfolding bribery probe by Chinese authorities into the U.K. drug maker has alarmed Western companies with business there that are accustomed to highly-publicized corruption crackdowns on Chinese officials, but who sees the Glaxo matter as new territory, China watchers said. The push against Glaxo could signal that a new anticorruption push in China could now also include foreign companies." I would suggest that an immediate review of your sales operations is in order. Matthews quoted Joe Warin, a partner at Gibson Dunn & Crutcher LLP, who said, "In particular, companies should examine relationships with travel agencies and event-planning companies, which have long been an "Achilles heel" in China". The first thing that you should check on is to see the spend that you have with any Chinese travel agencies. You should then match up all receipts and other documentation with all costs to see if there is anything out of line.

You should also look at your own employee base. Regarding a company's own employees, Matthew quoted Jerome Cohen, co-director of New York University School of Law's U.S.-Asia Law Institute, for the following, "This is a fairly obvious warning that companies need to conscientiously scrutinize the activities of their employees there". Remember the Eli Lilly and Company (Lilly) FCPA enforcement action brought by the SEC late last year? The bribery scheme which got Lilly into trouble in China involved its own employees, who inflated their expense accounts and used the extra money to pay bribes to secure sales.

It is clear that companies should follow Matthews' advice that "multinationals need to scour their operations in China to limit their vulnerability to future investigations." Now is the time to begin your own investigations because you certainly do not want to be like GSK and find out about allegations that your employees engaged in a multi-year, multi-million dollar bribery and corruption scheme through a public pronouncement from the Chinese Public Security Ministry.

Mike Volkov has provided information to the compliance practitioner to assist in this new world order in China. In a blog post, entitled "*China and Compliance Solutions: Choking Off the Money Supply*" and webinar, entitled "*How to Avoid Corruption Risks in China*", Volkov gave some specific suggestions for the compliance professional to utilize in the current enforcement environment in China. In his webinar, he said that western companies operating in China need to understand that the cost of compliance will exceed the amount spent in other countries. While there is certainly an upside in revenues from China business, it also involves greater compliance costs and risks. Companies need to construct enhanced compliance controls and implement aggressive monitoring programs, demand adherence to strict documentation policies and to integrate non-Chinese controls and personnel into China operations to supervise and monitor the local operations.

Volkov identified third party risks as the greatest risk because companies have a limited ability to control the outgoing expenditures of third parties than they do of their own. Some of the key questions that need to be explored in the due diligence process include what specific services will the third parties be providing and have you verified that the potential agent can deliver those services? You need to care that there is an absence of relationship between your Chinese employees and third party. You also need to inquire about how the third party came to your company's attention, for example does it have an internal sponsor in your company? Volkov notes that not only must audit rights be secured by western companies; they need to exercise those rights. Lastly, he advises that any unjustified expenditures have to be aggressively pursued both through the audit process and into the investigative process, if needed.

Additional questions you can ask, in the review of third parties who might provide such services, are:

- What is the ownership of the third party? Is there a business justification for the relationship?
- Is there anyone in the company who is responsible for maintaining the relationship?
- Is there ongoing accountability?
- How is the relationship being managed?
- Are you engaging in any transaction monitoring?
- Are you engaging in any relationship monitoring?
- What is the estimated or budgeted size of the spend with the third party?
- What do the actual spends show going forward?

Volkov believes that a key control involves focusing on internal expenditures. Unfortunately, he notes that external auditors often rely on Chinese affiliates, who he believes are "notorious for bending to company resistance to auditing standards and inquiries." Therefore companies need to require their external auditors to install quality controls. Companies should also demand strict adherence to auditing standards. He suggests that there should be both forensic auditing and transaction testing to review individual receipts and transactions. Lastly, he suggests that money should only be doled out through strict supervision by a non-Chinese controller.

In his blog post, Volkov drills down into some specific protections that a company can take to control its cash outlays in China to try and prevent some of the more well-known bribery schemes. He believes that "The strategy for compliance is then to focus on access to the money which the bribe payor needs to complete the bribe. Resources and controls need to be allocated and designed based on this analysis and focus." He provides a scenario where bribery and corruption can occur and a possible strategy to combat such actions.

In his scenario, an employee obtains company money by fraud and then pays a government official. The employee uses a fake invoice(s), which is typically required in China to satisfy tax authorities, and the fake invoice, which may involve another party as the recipient of the payment, is a means by which to "steal" the money from the company and use it for an improper purpose. This was the bribery scheme used by Lilly's employees in China where employees submitted false expense accounts and used the difference to fund their bribery scheme.

Volkov's proscription for this is that the company's compliance function must ensure that internal financial controls are scrupulously followed, so that any potential fake invoice is identified in advance. He believes whether the offender is an ex-pat or a local employee it is important to enforce such rules, it is an issue which can be debated and the outcome will depend on the personnel and the specific situation facing the company. The reason would seem rather self-obvious; that is, if no one is watching the invoicing process, verifying the accuracy of the invoice and ensuring that the payment is justified, money will slip out from the company for bribes. This means the focus of internal controls should include not only fake invoices but systems, procedures and forms to ensure that only approved and appropriate payments are made.

Chapter XVI - Due Diligence and the Management of Third Parties Going Forward in China

With the Humphrey and Yu convictions in China for performing investigations, a reasonable question that you might ask yourself is whether or not you can get adequate due diligence going forward in China for your anti-corruption compliance program? You should always remember that performing due diligence is but one of five steps in the management of the third party life cycle. If you cannot perform due diligence at a level that you do in other countries or that you could even have done in China before the Humphrey and Yu trial, you can beef up the other steps to help proactively manage your third parties. I often say that your real work with third parties begins when the contract is executed because then you have to manage the relationship going forward. So, if you cannot perform the level of due diligence you might like, you can put more resources into monitoring the relationship, particularly in the area of invoice review and payments going forward.

In the August 2014 SCCE magazine, Compliance and Ethics Professional, Dennis Hast and Caroline Lee published an article, entitled *"China clamps down on bribery and corruption: Why third-party due diligence is a necessity"*, where they discussed a more robust response to the issue as well. They note that the retention of third party's to do business in China is an established mechanism through which to conduct business. They advise "For multinationals with a Chinese presence, or plans to enter the market in the near future, now is the time to pay close attention to the changing nature of the business landscape as it relates to bribery and corruption." Further, they suggest that "In order to ensure compliance with ABAC [anti-bribery/anti-corruption] regulatory scrutiny, multinationals must demonstrate a consistent, intentional and systematic approach to third-party compliance." But in addition to the traditional background due diligence, they believe that companies should consider an approach that moves to proactively managing and monitoring third parties for compliance. Lastly, at the end of the day if a regulator comes knocking from the DOJ or SFO, you will need to demonstrate the steps you have put in place and your active management of the process.

One clear lesson that persons performing due diligence should strongly consider is based upon the convictions of Humphrey and Yu. Humphrey had previously said that he would not have taken on the GSK sex tape assignment if it had been disclosed to him that the company had sustained allegations of corruption by an internal whistleblower. If you are investigator it may be well incumbent on you to ask if the company is undergoing a corruption investigation or enforcement action. Perhaps another lesson might be that in the future companies will have to disclosure more to those they approach to perform such investigative services.

The more I think about the convictions of Peter Humphrey and his wife, for violating China's privacy laws regarding their investigation of who filmed the head of GSK's China unit head *in flagrante delicto* with his Chinese girlfriend, the more I consider the issue of risk in the management of third parties under the FCPA. In an article in the WSJ, entitled *"Chinese Case Lays Business Tripwires"*, reporters James T. Areddy and Laurie Burkitt explored some of the problems brought about by the investigators convictions.

They quoted Manuel Maisog, chief China representative for the law firm Hunton & Williams LLP, who summed up the problem regarding background due diligence investigations as "How can I do that in China?" Maisog went on to say, "The verdict created new uncertainties for doing business in China since the case hinged on the couple's admissions that they purchased personal information about Chinese citizens on behalf of clients. Companies in China may need to adjust how they assess future merger partners, supplier proposals or whether employees are involved in bribery."

I had pondered what that meant for a company that wanted to do business in China, through some type of third party relationship, from a sales representative to distributor to a joint venture (JV). What if you cannot get such information? How can you still have a *best practices* compliance program around third parties representatives if you cannot get information such as ultimate beneficial ownership? At a recent SCCE event, I put that question to a DOJ representative. Paraphrasing his response, he said that companies still need to ask the question in a due diligence questionnaire or other format. What if a third party refuses to answer, citing some national law against disclosure? His response was that a company needs to very closely weigh the risk of doing business with a party that refuses to identify its ownership.

The more that I thought about that answer the more I became convinced that it was not only the right answer under any type of FCPA compliance program but also the right response from a business perspective. A company must know who it is doing business with, for a wide variety of reasons. The current situation in China and even the convictions of Humphrey and Yu do not change this basic premise. You can *ask* the question. If a party does not want to disclose its ownership, you should consider this in any business relationship going forward.

The Humphrey and Yu conviction do not prevent you from asking the question about ownership. Their convictions mean that you may not be able to *verify* that information through what many people thought was publicly available information, at least publicly available in the west. I was struck by one line in the Areddy and Burkitt article, "It's not just that the tactical business practices need to change; it's the mind set" quoting again from Maisog.

I have broken down the management of third parties under the FCPA into five steps, they are:

1. Business Justification and Business Sponsor;
2. Questionnaire to Third Party;
3. Due Diligence on Third Party;
4. Compliance Terms and Conditions, including payment terms; and
5. Management and Oversight of Third Parties After Contract Signing.

The due diligence step is but one of these five. Further due diligence is performed in large part to verify the information that you receive back from a proposed third party. So what if you can no longer use avenues previously open to you in markets such as China? Perhaps there are other ways to manage this issue. Areddy and Burkitt also interviewed Jerry Ling, a partner at Jones Day, for the following "companies will need to analyze Chinese accounting documents themselves and conduct more in-person interviews with anyone they want to know more about in China."

Ling's point dovetails directly into what I heard from the DOJ representative. There is nothing about the Chinese law, or any other country's law, which prevents you from asking some basic questions that are found in Step 2 cited above. You can always ask who the owners of a company are, whether they are direct or beneficial. You can always ask if a company, its owners or its senior management have been involved in any incidents involving bribery and corruption and you can always ask if the company has a Code of Conduct and/or compliance program and whether its owners or senior management are aware of the FCPA and have had training on it.

Assuming the company will answer your questionnaire, the difficulty you may find yourself in now is verifying the information that you receive. In Ronald Reagan parlance, you may trust but you may not be able to verify it. Ling said in the WSJ article that "The challenge now for clients is that it's hard to get good information."

However, due diligence is but one step in the management of any third party in a FCPA compliance program. Just as when risk goes up and you increase your management around that risk, the situation is similar in here. Putting it another way, if you cannot obtain private information such as personal identification numbers during the due diligence process, you can put greater management around the other steps that you can take. Further, there has been nothing reported which would suggest that publicly filed corporate licenses or other information that might show ownership can no longer be accessed. Court records and public media searches also seem to still be available.

But what if you simply cannot determine if the information you are provided regarding ownership is accurate or even truthful? You can still work to manage the relationship through your commercial terms by setting your commission or other pay rates at a reasonable amount of scale. If you are dealing with a commissioned sales representative, you can probably manage this area of the relationship by setting the commission in the range of 5%. You can also manage the relationship by reviewing invoices to make sure there is an adequate description of the services provided so that they justify whatever compensation the third party is entitled to receive under the contract. You may also want to schedule such a third party for an audit ahead of other parties to help ensure adherence to your compliance terms and conditions.

There may be times when you cannot verify the true or ultimate beneficial owner of a third party. That does not have to be the end of the analysis. If that situation arises, you may want to see if there are other risk mitigation tools at your disposal. Put another way, if such a red flag arises, can it be cleared? Can it be managed? If your company is looking at a major deal for multi-millions and your agent will receive a six or seven figure commission, the risk of not knowing with certainty may be too great because in such a case, an unknown owner could be a government official who has awarded the contract. But if your agent receives a considerably smaller commission and hence there is a considerably small amount of money to constitute a bribe, you may be able to manage that risk through a close and effective relationship management process.

Chapter XVII - Business Lessons from GSK

The DOJ and SEC have made it abundantly clear over the past several years that companies should assess their risk and then manage their own risks. In the anti-corruption space, simply putting in a *Check-the-Box* paper compliance program does not help to prevent, detect or remediate under laws such as the FCPA or UK Bribery Act. In their joint FCPA Guidance, the DOJ and SEC make clear there are a variety of steps a company can take to manage anti-corruption risks.

One of the tired excuses for cutting back on FCPA enforcement is that it costs US companies business overseas because they cannot engage in bribery and corruption, while the commercial enterprises of countries which do not have robust anti-corruption laws essentially bribe at will. However, there are many business solutions available in the management of risk, which companies can profitably use to help ameliorate bribery and corruption risk.

In an article in the FT, entitled *"Witty comes out fighting for GSK"*, Andrew Ward reviewed some of the business responses that GSK has contemplated over the past year since the revelations about allegations of bribery in China. Ward reported that in addition to the uncertainty of the ongoing corruption investigation by Chinese authorities, the SFO for violations of the UK Bribery Act and the DOJ for violations of the FCPA; the company "issued a profits warning that exposed weakness in the company's core respiratory medicines business." These warnings turned on "the decline in the company's best selling drug. Revenues from Advair, an asthma treatment that accounts for a fifth of sales, fell 12 per cent in the second quarter, on top of the 15 per cent drop in the three months before that." Moreover, the company's stock is down some 14% in the past year.

I was intrigued by the response of GSK CEO Sir Andrew Witty. He did not bemoan the corruption investigations that his company is going through or somehow try to claim that the company simply could not compete because of the scrutiny it is under. On the business front Ward reported, "GSK's innovation engine is working" as Witty noted that the company had "six new drugs approved across all therapeutic areas last year and a further 40 in advanced development".

In addition to the specific response regarding the development of new pharmaceutical products, Witty is looking at other sales products and models that will lessen the company's corruption risk while providing a strong business base. Ward reported that Witty is "strengthening GSK's two other businesses: vaccines and healthcare." This move "was reinforced by a $20bn asset swap with Novartis in April under which GSK traded its subscale oncology business for the Swiss group's vaccines division, while the pair agreed to set up a joint-venture in consumer products." This means that when this structuring is completed, "half of GSK's revenues will come from outside [the sale of] pharmaceuticals."

Witty has also worked to change internal GSK compensation incentives to help manage corruption risks. Late last year, the company announced that it would "sever the link between sales and pay for drug reps and from 2016, stop payments to doctors for promoting its products." Ward noted that others in the industry have not followed GSK's lead in changing the way it compensates its sales team but Witty said, "in the long-run, the company will benefit from being the first-mover towards a new marketing model."

Finally, and perhaps most interestingly, Witty has attempted to become an industry-wide "standard-bearer for [pharmaceutical] industry ethics." Ward reported that the ongoing scandal has helped Witty "drive home to employees the need for greater transparency." Ward even quoted Witty for the following, "It gives me the ammunition to say we are in the public eye and our behaviour counts. It's not just about generating prescriptions, it's how you do it."

In another article on the GSK corruption scandal by Ward, entitled "*GSK chief floats break-up option*", Ward said that Witty has "zero tolerance for any form of corruption" and that "he was pleased if wrongdoing had been brought to light so that it could be stamped out." Witty went on to say that "Any company that doesn't get whistleblower letters isn't looking hard enough. If you are not getting any don't dream. It can't be perfect 100 per cent of the time." But this promises to be a long rebuilding process and for GSK the process will largely be rebuilding trust rather than maximizing profits.

Another perspective on business solutions to the management of corruption risks came from Tom Mitchell, also writing in the FT in an article entitled "*Expats in China should read GSK potboiler carefully*". Mitchell focused on a book by Joe Studwell called *The China Dream*, which detailed some of the business failures that had befallen western companies in China. Mitchell drew the lesson from Studwell's book that "When foreign investors' interests are aligned with those of their domestic partners – as they generally are today in the auto sector – those investors do very well indeed… However, when interests are not aligned - or when outside operators in sectors where they are not required to have joint ventures - foreigners are vulnerable to sudden reversals of fortune instigated by either a bitter partner or by unsympathetic officials."

How closely does that sound like what happened to GSK? Mitchell noted that GSK "made money from selling goods in China at prices that were - Chinese police allege - high by the standards of many markets. At the same time, GSK was not sharing revenue streams with a local partner that could help with damage limitation when local authorities appeared on its doorstep."

The management of risk is essentially a business exercise. That is because risk is what can cause a company to lose money. Some legal risk is embodied in statutes such as the FCPA or UK Bribery Act. Sometimes risk is a change in the market circumstance. Yet GSK may well come out the other side of the Chinese corruption scandal stronger because they seem to understand that there is a market based solution to corruption risks. GSK has changed the way it will compensate its sales force and will delete its compensation to doctors. This may take away incentives to cut corners or engage in bribery and corruption. But think about Witty's steps to diversify the GSK product base. If you are in an industry that is corrupt and you cannot find a way to do business profitably, your company may have other business lines it can move forward to a more prominent role in your business. Lastly, as with most responses to legal issues by lawyers, business executives are only limited by their imaginations in their response to business issues.

Chapter XVIII - Board of Directors and Doing Business in China

While many questions are still unanswered, one that seems to be at the forefront was where were the GSK Board of Directors during the investigation phase of this matter? The role of a Board of Directors is becoming more important and more of a critical part of any effective compliance program. Indeed Board involvement is listed as one of the ten hallmarks of an effective compliance program as set out in the 2012 FCPA Guidance. In addition to helping to set the proper tone in an organization, the Board has a specific oversight role in any FCPA or UK Bribery Act compliance program.

A. Some Case Law

As to the specific role of *best practices* in the area of general compliance and ethics, one can look to Delaware corporate law for guidance. The case of *In Re Caremark International Inc. Derivative Litigation 698 A.2d 959 (Del.1996)* was the first case to hold that a Board's obligation "includes a duty to attempt in good faith to assure that a corporate information and reporting system, which the board concludes is adequate, exists, and that failure to do so under some circumstances may, in theory at least, render a director liable for losses caused by non-compliance with applicable legal standards." The Corporate Compliance Blog, in a post entitled "*Caremark 101*", said that the Caremark case "addressed the board's duty to oversee a corporation's legal compliance efforts. As part of its duty to monitor, the Board must make good faith efforts to ensure that a corporation has adequate reporting and information systems. The opinion described this claim as "possibly the most difficult theory in corporation law upon which a plaintiff might hope to win a judgment," with liability attaching only for "a sustained or systematic failure to exercise oversight" or "[a]n utter failure to attempt to ensure a reporting and information system.""

In the case of *Stone v. Ritter 911 A.2d 362, 370 (Del. 2006)*, the Supreme Court of Delaware expanded on the Caremark decision by establishing two important principles. First, the Court held that the Caremark standard is the appropriate standard for director duties with respect to corporate compliance issues. Second, the Court found that there is no duty of good faith that forms a basis, independent of the duties of care and loyalty, for director liability. Rather, *Stone v. Ritter* holds that the question of director liability turns on whether there is a "sustained or systematic failure of the board to exercise oversight – such as an utter failure to attempt to assure a reasonable information and reporting system exists."

Andrew J. Demetriou and Jessica T. Olmon, writing in the ABA Health Esource blog, said that "This standard aims to protect shareholders by ensuring that corporations will adopt reasonable programs to deter, detect and address violations of law and corporate policy, while absolving the Board from liability for corporate conduct so long as it has exercised reasonable responsibility with respect to the adoption and maintenance of a compliance and reporting system. Although the standard protects the Board, consistent with most jurisprudence under the business judgment rule, it also requires that the Board follow through to address problems of which it has notice and this may include adopting modifications to its compliance program to address emerging risks."

Lastly, I recently heard well-known conflicts of interest expert Jeff Kaplan discuss the oversight obligations of the Board regarding the compliance function. In addition to the above cases, he discussed the case of *Louisiana Municipal Police Employees' Retirement System et al. v. David Pyott, et al., 2012 WL 2087205 (Del. Ch. June 11, 2012)* (rev'd on other grounds, No. 380, 2012, 2013 WL 1364695 (Del. Apr. 4, 2013)*), which was a shareholder action that went forward against a Board based upon a claim that the Board knew of compliance risk based on the company's business plan. The Delaware Court pointed out the possibility that "The appearance of formal compliance cloaked the reality of noncompliance, and directors who understood the difference between legal off-label sales and illegal off-label marketing continued to approve and oversee business plans that depended on illegal activity." Kaplan believes this case, more generally, supports the need for risk-based oversight by board. Finally, is the ongoing shareholder litigation around Wal-Mart's FCPA investigation into in Mexico subsidiaries bribery. This may lead to additional Board obligations around compliance.

B. FCPA Guidance and US Sentencing Guidelines

In the Ten Hallmarks of an Effective Compliance Program, set out in the FCPA Guidance, there are two specific references to the obligations of a Board. The first in Hallmark No. 1, entitled *"Commitment from Senior Management and a Clearly Articulated Policy Against Corruption"*, states "Within a business organization, compliance begins with the board of directors and senior executives setting the proper tone for the rest of the company." The second is found under Hallmark No. 3, entitled *"Oversight, Autonomy and Resources"*, where it discussed that the Chief Compliance Officer (CCO) should have "direct access to an organization's governing authority, such as the board of directors and committees of the board of directors (e.g., the audit committee)." Additionally, under the US Sentencing Guidelines, a Board must exercise reasonable oversight on the effectiveness of a company's compliance program. The DOJ's Prosecution Standards posed the following queries: (1) Do the Directors exercise independent review of a company's compliance program? and (2) Are Directors provided information sufficient to enable the exercise of independent judgment?

Board failure to heed this warning can lead to serious consequences. David Stuart, a senior attorney with Cravath, Swaine & Moore LLP, noted that FCPA compliance issues can lead to personal liability for directors, as both the SEC and DOJ have been "very vocal about their interest in identifying the highest-level individuals within the organization who are responsible for the tone, culture, or weak internal controls that may contribute to, or at least fail to prevent, bribery and corruption". He added that based upon the SEC's enforcement action against two senior executives at Nature's Sunshine Products, "Under certain circumstances, I could see the SEC invoking the same provisions against audit committee members—for instance, for failing to oversee implementation of a compliance program to mitigate risk of bribery". It would not be too far a next step for the SEC to invoke the same provisions against audit committee members who do not actively exercise oversight of an ongoing compliance program.

There is one other issue regarding the Board and risk management, including FCPA risk management, which should be noted. It appears that the SEC desires Boards to take a more active role in overseeing the management of risk within a company. The SEC has promulgated Regulation SK 407 under which each company must make a disclosure regarding the Board's role in risk oversight which "may enable investors to better evaluate whether the board is exercising appropriate oversight of risk." If this disclosure is not made, it could be a securities law violation and subject the company, which fails to disclose it, to fines, penalties or profit disgorgement.

In addition to the pronouncements set out in the FCPA Guidance, other commentators have discussed the legal duties set out for Board members regarding compliance. Donna Boehme, writing in the SCCE Complete Compliance and Ethics Manual, 2nd Ed., entitled *"Board Engagement, Training and Reporting: Strategies for the Chief Ethics and Compliance Officer"*, said that these state court decisions establish the parameters of Board duty of care for corporate compliance activities. Moreover, this case law on the duty of a Board member, read in conjunction with the US Sentencing Guidelines, set out the elements of an effective program to be overseen by the Board. The US Sentencing Guidelines also require that a Board "be "knowledgeable" about the content and operation of the company program and exercise "reasonable oversight" over its implementation and effectiveness."

C. Boards and Operations in China

In a NACD Directorship article, entitled *"Corruption in China and Elsewhere Demands Board Oversight"*, Eric Zwisler and Dean Yoost noted that as "Boards are ultimately responsible for risk oversight" any Board of a company with operations in China "needs to have a clear understanding of its duties and responsibilities under the FCPA and other international laws, such as the U.K. Bribery Act". Why should China be on the radar of Boards? The authors reported that "20 percent of FCPA enforcement actions in the past five years have involved business conduct in China. The reputational and economic ramifications of misinterpreting these duties and responsibilities can have a long-lasting impact on the economic and reputation of the company."

The authors understand that corruption can be endemic in China. They wrote that "Local organizations in China are exceedingly adept at appearing compliant while hiding unacceptable business practices. The board should be aware that a well-crafted compliance program must be complemented with a thorough understanding of frontline business practices and constant auditing of actual practices, not just documentation." Further, "the management cadence of monitoring and auditing should be visible to the board." Echoing one of the Board's roles, as articulated in the FCPA Guidance, the authors considered that a "board must ensure that the human resources committed to compliance management and reporting relationships are commensurate with the level of compliance risk." So if that risk is perceived to be high in a country, such as China, the Board should follow the prescription in the Guidance which states "the amount of resources devoted to compliance will depend on the company's size, complexity, industry, geographical reach, and risks associated with the business. In assessing whether a company has reasonable internal controls, DOJ and SEC typically consider whether the company devoted adequate staffing and resources to the compliance program given the size, structure, and risk profile of the business."

To help achieve these goals, the authors suggested a list of questions that they believe every director should ask about a company's business in China.

- How is "tone at the top" established and communicated?
- How are business practice risks assessed?
- Are effective standards, policies and procedures in place to address these risks?
- What procedures are in place to identify and mitigate fraud, theft, corruption?
- What local training is conducted on business practices and is it effective?
- Are incentives provided to promote the correct behaviors?
- How is the detection of improper behavior monitored and audited?
- How is the effectiveness of the compliance program reviewed and initiated?
- If a problem is identified, how is an independent and thorough investigation assured?

The authors correctly pointed out that third parties generally present the most risk under a FCPA compliance program and that "more than 90 percent of reported FCPA cases involve the use of third-party intermediaries such as agents or consultants." However, they also noted that "all potential opportunities in China will have some level of compliance related issues." As JVs and the acquisition of Chinese entities are an important component of many organizations' strategic plans in China, it is important to have Board oversight in the mergers and acquisition (M&A) process.

The authors understand that "non-compliant business practices and how to bring these into compliance is often a major and defining deal risk." But, more importantly, it is a company's "inability to understand actual business practices, the impact of those practices on the core business, and effectively dealing with a transition plan is one of the main reasons why joint ventures and acquisitions fail." So even if the conduct of an acquisition target was legal or tolerated in its home country, once that target is acquired and subject to the FCPA or Bribery Act, such conduct must stop. However, if such conduct ends, it may so devalue the core assets of the acquired entity so as to ruin the business basis for the transaction. The authors cited back to the FCPA Guidance and its prescribed due diligence in the pre-acquisition stage as a key to this dilemma. But those guidelines also make clear that post-acquisition integration is a must to avoid FCPA liability if the illegal conduct continues after the transaction is completed.

The authors concluded by articulating that many Boards are not engaged enough to understand the way that their company is conducting business, particularly in a business environment as challenging as China. They believe that a Board should have a "detailed understanding of the business if it is to be an effective safeguard against fraud or corrupt practices." They remind us that not only should a Board understand the specific financial risks to a company if a FCPA violation is uncovered; but perhaps more importantly the "potential impact on the corporate culture and the risk to the company's reputation, including the reputations of individual board members." Finally, the authors stated that "effective oversight of corruption in China will only become increasingly more important". That may be the most important lesson for any Board collective or Board member individually to take away from the GSK corruption and bribery scandal.

Chapter XIX - More Compliance Lessons

A. Integrating Your Risk Assessment

One of the things that a compliance program must have is the flexibility to respond to changing events on the ground. Just as the GSK corruption scandal in China brought attention to domestic prosecutions of corruption in China, these very public events should bring the attention of your compliance team. My former *This Week in FCPA* co-host Howard Sklar said that a compliance program needed to be nimble and agile enough in order to respond to such events in far-flung places. Risks change and they must be evaluated on a regular basis or in response to new facts on the ground, such as those which are present in China.

There may also be more than anti-corruption risk at play in any given situation. If a company only looks at one type of risk, such as anti-corruption, rather than others such as export control or anti-money laundering (AML) it can lead to the concept of what is called the "functional trap" of labeling and compartmentalizing risk. In an article in the June 2014 issue of the Harvard Business Review (HBR), entitled "*Managing Risks: A New Framework*", authors Robert Kaplan and Annette Mikes declare that good risk discussions must be integrative in order for risk interaction to be evaluated. If not, a business "can be derailed by a combination of small events that reinforce one another in unanticipated ways."

The authors posit that it is difficult for companies to accurately and adequately discuss risk for a variety of reasons. One of these reasons is the aforementioned silo effect which can lead to a lack of discussion by a wide group regarding a number of risks, for example compliance risk; reputational risk; brand risk; credit risk and human resources risk are but a few of the types of risks mentioned in their article. The authors believe that one of the ways to knock down these silos when it comes to a more complete management of risk is to "anchor their discussions in strategic planning, one integrative process that most well-run companies already have" in place.

The authors cautioned that beyond simply introducing a systematic process for identifying and mitigating key risks, companies should also employ a risk oversight structure. The authors discussed the experience of the Indian IT company, Infosys, which uses a dual structure. It consists of a central team that identifies general strategy risks and then establishes central policy, together with a specialized, decentralized functional team. This second team designs and monitors policies and controls in consultation with local business units. These decentralized teams have the authority and expertise to respond to changes in the company's risk profile coupled with the nimbleness and agility of being in the field to deal with smaller issues before they become larger problems for the central team back in the corporate office.

I believe that the current political turmoil in China provides an example of the diversity your compliance program and risk assessment must maintain. Just as it is important to perform due diligence on third party representatives, before execution of an appropriate contract, the real work is in managing the relationship. In risk management, you must identify and assess the risk but the real work begins in managing the risk. This is where the rubber meets the road.

B. Board Oversight and Tone in the Middle

What are some of the lessons to be learned from GSK in China regarding the role of a company's Board of Directors and 'tone in the middle'? While we have not heard from the GSK Board on this case, it has become clear that the GSK Board was aware of both the anonymous whistleblower allegations and the release of the sex tape of the GSK China Country Manager and his girlfriend. One of the lessons learned from the GSK scandal is that a Board must absolutely take a more active oversight role not only when specific allegations of bribery and corruption are brought forward but also when companies are operating in high risk environments. Clearly this will be a major task for incoming Board Chairman, Sir Philip Hamilton, who joined the Board in January 2015 and will become the Chairman, later in the year when a successor is found for his current position as Chairman at the Royal Bank of Scotland.

One of the major failings of the GSK Board was that it apparently did not understand the actual business practices that the company was engaging in through its China business unit. While $500MM may not have been a material monetary figure for the Board to consider; the payment of such an amount to any third party or group of third parties, such as Chinese travel agencies, should have been raised to the Board. All of this leads me to believe that the GSK Board was not sufficiently engaged. While one might think a company which had received a $3bn fine and was under a CIA for its marketing sins might have sufficient Board attention; perhaps legal marketing had greater Board scrutiny than doing business in compliance with the FCPA or UK Bribery Act. The Board certainly did not seem to understand the potential financial and reputational impact of a bribery and corruption matter arising in China. Perhaps they do now but, for the rest of us, I think the clear lesson to be learned is that a Board must increase oversight of its China operations from the anti-corruption perspective.

GSK CEO Sir Andrew Witty has certainly tried to say all of the right things during the GSK imbroglio on China. But did that message really get down into to the troops at GSK China? Moreover, did that message even get to middle management, such as the GSK leadership in China? Apparently not so, one of the lessons learned is moving the Olympian Pronouncements of Witty down to lower levels of his company. Just how important is "Tone at the Top"? Conversely, what does it say to middle management when upper management practices the age-old parental line of "Don't do as I do; Do as I say"? In his article entitled *"Ethics and the Middle Manager: Creating "Tone in The Middle"*, Kirk O. Hanson listed eight specific actions that top executives could engage in which demonstrate a company's and their personnel's commitment to ethics and compliance. The actions he listed were:

1. Top executives must themselves exhibit all the "tone at the top" behaviors, including acting ethically, talking frequently about the organization's values and ethics, and supporting the organization's and individual employee's adherence to the values.
2. Top executives must explicitly ask middle managers what dilemmas arise in implementing the ethical commitments of the organization in the work of that group.
3. Top executives must give general guidance about how values apply to those specific dilemmas.
4. Top executives must explicitly delegate resolution of those dilemmas to the middle managers.
5. Top executives must make it clear to middle managers that their ethical performance is being watched as closely as their financial performance.
6. Top executives must make ethical competence and commitment of middle managers a part of their performance evaluation.
7. The organization must provide opportunities for middle managers to work with peers on resolving the hard cases.
8. Top executives must be available to the middle managers to discuss/coach/resolve the hardest cases.

What about at the bottom, as in remember those China unit employees who claimed they were owed bonuses because their bosses had *instructed* them to pay bribes? Well if your management instructs you to pay bribes that is a very different problem. But if your company's issue is how to move the message of compliance down to the bottom, Dawn Lomer, Managing Editor at i-Sight.com, a compliance related software provider, related some concrete suggestions in a SCCE magazine article, entitled "*An ethical corporate culture goes beyond the code*", where she wrote that that the unofficial message which a company sends to its employees "is just as powerful - if not more powerful - than any messages carried in the code of conduct." Lomer suggested that a company use "unofficial channels" by which it can convey and communicate its message regarding doing business in an ethical manner and "influence employee behavior across the board." Her suggestions were:

1. *Reward for Integrity* - Lomer writes that the key is to reward employees for doing business in an ethical manner and that such an action "sends a powerful message without saying a word."
2. *The three-second ethics rule* - It is important that senior management not only consistently drives home the message of doing business ethically but they should communicate that message in a short, clear values statement.
3. *Environmental cues* - Simply the idea that a company is providing oversight on doing business ethically can be enough to modify employee behavior.
4. *Control the images* - It is not all about winning but conducting business, as it should be done.

5. *Align Messages* - You should think about the totality of the messages that your company is sending out to its employees regarding doing business and make sure that all these messages are aligned in a way that makes clear your ethical corporate culture clear.

The GSK case will be in the public eye for many months to come. Both the SFO and US authorities have open investigations into the company. Just as the five counter-point singing or the rooftop symphonic dance scene to the song *America* demonstrates the best of that art form; you can draw lessons from GSK's missteps in China now for implementing or enhancing your anti-corruption compliance program going forward now.

C. Internal Investigations

One of the clear lessons from the GSK matter is that serious allegations of bribery and corruption require a serious corporate response. Not, as GSK did in their best Inspector Clouseau imitation by failing to find the nose on their face. I was particularly focused on GSK's response to at least two separate reports from an anonymous whistleblower (brilliantly monikered as *GSK Whistleblower)* of allegations of bribery and corruption going on in the company's China business unit.

Further, and more nefariously, is GSK's documented treatment of and history with internal whistleblowers. One can certainly remember GSK whistleblower Cheryl Eckard. In a 2010 article in The Guardian by Graeme Wearden, entitled *"GlaxoSmithKline whistleblower awarded $96m payout"*, he reported that Eckard was fired by the company "after repeatedly complaining to GSK's management that some drugs made at Cidra were being produced in a non-sterile environment, that the factory's water system was contaminated with micro-organisms, and that other medicines were being made in the wrong doses." She later was awarded $96MM as her share of the settlement of a Federal Claims Act whistleblower lawsuit. Eckard was quoted as saying, "It's difficult to survive this financially, emotionally, you lose all your friends, because all your friends are people you have at work. You really do have to understand that it's a very difficult process but very well worth it." So to think that GSK may simply have been SHOCKED, SHOCKED, that allegations of corruption were brought by an internal whistleblower may well be within the realm of accurate.

There would have seemed to have been plenty of evidence to let the company know that something askance was going on in its Chinese operations. The international press was certainly able to make that connection early on in the scandal. Remember the GSK sales strategy code-named *Vasily?* From my experience, if you have a bribery scheme that has its own code name, even if you never implemented that scheme, it probably means that the propensity for such is pervasive throughout the system. So even if the company believes a code named illegal scheme was not ever put in place, it certainly is a red flag indicating that a more robust follow-up is warranted.

I have often written about the need for a company to have an investigative protocol in place so that it is not making up its process in the face of a crisis. However the GSK matter does not appear to be that situation. It would not have mattered what investigation protocol GSK followed, it would seem they were determined not to find any evidence of bribery and corruption in their China business unit. So the situation is more likely that GSK should have brought in a competent investigation expert law firm to head up their investigation in the face of this anonymous whistleblower's allegations.

In an ACC Docket article, entitled *"Risks and Rewards of an Independent Investigation"*, authors James McGrath and David Hildebrandt discuss the use of *specialized* outside counsel to lead an independent internal investigation as compliance and ethics *best practices*. This is based upon the US Sentencing Guidelines, under which a scoring system is utilized to determine what a final sentence should be for a criminal act. Factors taken into account include the type of offense involved and the severity of the said offense, as well as the harm produced. Additional points are either added or subtracted for mitigating factors. One of the mitigating factors can be whether an organization had an effective compliance and ethics program. McGrath and Hildebrandt argue that a company must have a robust internal investigation.

McGrath and Hildebrandt take this analysis a step further in urging that a company, when faced with an issue such as an alleged FCPA violation, should engage *specialized* counsel to perform the investigation. There were three reasons for this suggestion. The first is that the DOJ would look towards the independence and impartiality of such investigations as one of its factors in favor of declining or deferring enforcement. If in-house counsel were heading up the investigation, the DOJ might well deem the investigative results "less than trustworthy".

Matthew Goldstein and Barry Meier discussed the need for independence from the company being investigated in an article the NYT about the General Motors (GM) internal investigation entitled *"G.M Calls the Lawyers"*. They quoted William McLucas, a partner at WilmerHale, who said, "If you are a firm that is generating substantial fees from a prospective corporate client, you may be able to come in and do a bang-up inquiry. But the perception is always going to be there; maybe you pulled your punches because there is a business relationship." This is because if "companies want credibility with prosecutors and investors, it is generally not wise to use their regular law firms for internal inquiries." Another expert, Charles Elson, a professor of finance at the University of Delaware who specializes in corporate governance, agreed adding, "I would not have done it because of the optics. Public perception can be affected by using regular outside counsel.""

Adam G. Safwat, a former deputy chief of the fraud section in the Justice Department, said that the key is "Prosecutors expect an internal investigation to be an honest assessment of a company's misdeeds or faults, "What you want to avoid is doing something that will make the prosecutor question the quality of integrity of the internal investigation."" Also quoted was Internal Investigations Blog editor, Jim McGrath who said, "A shrewd law firm that gets out in front of scandal can use that to its advantage in negotiating with authorities to lower penalties and sanctions. There is a great incentive to ferret out information so they can spin it."

D. Internal Controls, Auditing and Monitoring

There are valuable lessons to be drawn from GSK's missteps in China around internal controls, auditing and monitoring an anti-corruption compliance program. One of the questions that GSK will have to face during the next few years of bribery and corruption investigations is how a massive bribery and corruption scheme occurred in its Chinese operations? The numbers went upwards of $500MM, which coincidentally was the amount of the fine levied by the Chinese court on GSK. It is not as if the Chinese medical market was not well known for its propensity towards corruption, as prosecutions of the FCPA are littered with the names of US companies which came to corruption grief in China. GSK itself seemed to be aware of the corruption risks in China. In his Reuters article Hirschler reported that the company had "more compliance officers in China than in any country bar the United States". Further, the company conducted "up to 20 internal audits in China a year, including an extensive 4-month probe earlier in 2013." GSK even had PwC as its outside auditor in China. Nevertheless, he noted, "GSK bosses were blindsided by police allegations of massive corruption involving travel agencies used to funnel bribes to doctors and officials."

1. Internal Controls

Where were the appropriate internal controls? You might think that a company as large as GSK and one that had gone through the ringer of a prior DOJ investigation resulting in charges for off-label marketing and an attendant CIA might have such controls in place. It was not as if the types of bribery schemes in China were not well known.

It would be reasonable to expect that internal controls over gifts would be designed to ensure that all gifts satisfy the required criteria, as defined and interpreted in Company policies. It should fall to a Compliance Officer to finalize and approve a definition of permissible and non-permissible gifts, travel and entertainment and internal controls will follow from such definition or criteria set by the company. These criteria would include the amount of the money spent, localized down into increased risk such as the higher risk recognized in China. Within this context, noted internal controls expert Henry Mixon has suggested the following specific controls. (1) Is the correct level of person approving the payment / reimbursement? (2) Are there specific controls (and signoffs) that the gift had proper business purpose? (3) Are the controls regarding gifts sufficiently preventative, rather than relying on detect controls? (4) If controls are not followed, is that failure detected?

2. Auditing

Following Mixon's point 4 above, what can or should be a company's response if one country's gifts, travel and entertainment expenses were kept 'off the books'? Put another way, what if you have systemic corruption by a business unit? This is where internal audit or outside auditors are critical. The situation that GSK corporate faced was fraud on a massive scale by its Chinese business unit. Further, from the conviction of the GSK Country Manager and other top China business unit executives and the claims by China unit rank and file for reinstatement of their bonuses and pay raises, it appears that the bribery and corruption was ingrained in the way the Chinese unit conducted itself. That is one of the reasons audit is such a key function in a *best practices* compliance regime. There is a clear need for oversight from a disinterested group outside of the business unit itself. This is segregation of duties at its most basic level. With all the information available about the nefarious uses of travel agencies, literally as 'cash machines' in China, GSK's auditors should have looked more closely on marketing expenses and more particularly, the monies spent on travel agencies.

But more than simply having internal or even external audit is the issue of materiality. Many internal auditors have not been trained that there is no materiality standard under the FCPA. This can lead to a large number of payments or even categories of payments being skipped over in such a review. So the individual payments involved, either by one or more employees or to one or more travel agencies, might not have registered as significant and bearing further scrutiny to an untrained internal auditor. Moreover, if more than one auditor is involved they may lack the continuity to understand the total aggregate of overall payments made to travel agencies in China.

3. Ongoing Monitoring

A final lesson is monitoring. As Stephen Martin often says, many compliance practitioners confuse auditing with monitoring. Monitoring is a commitment to reviewing and detecting compliance programs in real time and then reacting quickly to remediate them. A primary goal of monitoring is to identify and address gaps in your program on a regular and consistent basis. Auditing is a more limited review that targets a specific business component, region, or market sector during a particular timeframe in order to uncover and/or evaluate certain risks.

Here I want to focus on two types of ongoing monitoring. The first is relationship monitoring, performed by companies, such Boston-based Catelas, through software products. This would have been useful because Chinese business unit employees were reported to have used their personal email addresses to try and avoid detection of their communications. These software products leverage social network analysis and behavioral science algorithms to analyze communications data. These interactions are used to uncover and display the networks that exist within companies and between the employees of companies. Additionally, relationships between employees and external parties such as private webmail users, competitors and other parties can be uncovered. This might have been one tool that GSK could have used to monitor its own employees on an ongoing basis.

The second type of monitoring is transaction monitoring. Generally speaking, transaction monitoring involves review of large amounts of data. The analysis can be compared against an established norm which is derived either against a businesses' own standard or an accepted industry standard. If a payment, distribution or other financial payment made is outside an established norm, thus creating a red flag that can be tagged for further investigation.

GSK's failure in these three areas now seems self-evident. However, the company's foibles can be useful for the compliance practitioner in assessing where their company might be in these same areas. Moreover, as within any anti-corruption enforcement action, you can bet your bottom dollar that the regulators will be assessing *best practices* going forward based upon some or all of GSK's missteps going forward.

Chapter XX - Is a Country Sweep Coming to China?

A. What is a sweep under the FCPA?

The FCPA Professor, in a blog post entitled *"Industry Sweeps"*, posted an article from FCPA Dean Homer Moyer, entitled *"The Big Broom of FCPA Industry Sweeps"*. In his article, Moyer said that an industry sweep is the situation where the DOJ and/or SEC will focus "on particular industries – pharmaceuticals and medical devices come to mind — industry sweeps are investigations that grow out of perceived FCPA violations by one company that enforcement agencies believe may reflect an industry-wide pattern of wrongdoing." Moyer further wrote, "Industry sweeps are often led by the Securities and Exchange Commission ("SEC"), which has broad subpoena power as a regulatory agency, arguably broader oversight authority than prosecutors. They are different from internal investigations or traditional government investigations, and present different challenges to companies. Because the catalyst may be wrongdoing in a single company, agencies may have no evidence or suspicion of specific violations in the companies subject to an industry sweep. A sweep may thus begin with possible cause, not probable cause. In sweeps, agencies broadly solicit information from companies about their past FCPA issues or present practices. And they may explicitly encourage companies to volunteer incriminating information about competitors."

B. China Sweeps Itself?

As bad as a DOJ/SEC country sweep of China might seem to western companies, it might well blanch next to a sweep by Chinese authorities. Whether this is based on politics, nationalism, the rising cost of domestic drugs, anti-competitive practices or any other reason, it really does not matter. In a FT article, entitled *"China drug bribe probes broaden"*, reporters Patti Waldmeir, Jamil Anderlini and Andrew Jack wrote that Chinese authorities are widening their probe of western pharmaceutical companies. One example they cited was that the government of Shanghai "told hospitals to look for corruption in the purchasing and prescribing of drugs, as well as in clinical trials conducted with hospital participation." This broadening also included investigations of doctors. Separately the State Administration for Industry and Commerce announced that it would investigate "bribery, fraud and anti-competitive practices in a range of industries that touch the lives of consumers, from drugs and medical services to school admissions."

As the number of companies either being investigated in China or engaging in their own internal investigations increases Homer Moyer's statement that "Inevitably, industry sweeps become organic and evolve, with government investigators using information from one company as the basis for additional requests to others" may well omniscient. So in addition to the DOJ and SEC perhaps taking a different tack than simply focusing on one industry and starting a China sweep; the Chinese themselves may take up the task. If so there will most probably be cooperation between the various investigative agencies involved. All of that means more pain for the companies involved.

Chapter XXI - One More Nail in the Coffin of a Compliance Defense

I believe that one of the side effects from the GSK matter will be that one more nail is driven into the coffin of amending the FCPA to add a compliance defense. I find it amazing that some commentators are still arguing for amendment of the FCPA to add such an affirmative defense. A post on the FCPA Blog by Philip Fitzgerald, entitled *"From Europe, the case for an FCPA good-faith defense"*, posits that enforcement of foreign bribery in the US is effective under the FCPA because such enforcement is aided by the doctrine of *respondeat superior*. Fitzgerald then argues that a good-faith compliance defense has been considered for some time as a potential counterweight to *respondeat superior*. The reason being that if companies had incentives for effective compliance programs and were "accused of violating the FCPA could mount a defense based on their efforts to prevent the bribery are evident. Corporations accused of violating the FCPA would have access to courts and jury trials to contest and challenge FCPA allegations, would probably be encouraged to discover and self-report overseas bribery, and may not feel compelled to enter into settlements with enforcement agencies that can prejudice the rights of both the organizations and their employees."

Here is the problem with that argument. It apparently makes no difference what the incentives will be for a company to put a compliance program in place. For even if you have a compliance program it still has to be effective. Last year this was driven home by Wal-Mart and its allegations of wide spread bribery and corruption in its Mexico subsidiary. This year we have GSK running amok with allegations that it engaged in bribery and corruption in its Chinese operations.

A. The Uselessness of a Compliance Defense

So how does all of this portend the end of efforts to add a compliance defense to the FCPA? As stated in its Code of Conduct, "The GSK attitude towards corruption in all its forms is simple: it is one of zero tolerance." What do you think a compliance defense would do for GSK about now? GSK prided itself on its world-wide FCPA anti-corruption compliance program. It even said it would do so in settlement documents with the DOJ. The claim that companies would act more ethically and in compliance if they could rely on a compliance defense would seem to be negated by facts reported about GSK. Do these facts seem like a rogue employee or even junta of rogue China subsidiary employees going off on their own? Whatever your thoughts on that question may be, it certainly appears that having a *best practices* compliance program did not lead to GSK doing business more ethically. And what if GSK's corporate headquarters in London was not involved in any illegal conduct or were even kept in the dark by GSK China? What does that say about having a robust compliance program?

Amending the FCPA to protect corporate headquarters in the US from liability under the doctrine of *respondeat superior?* At this point, I do not think that anyone can argue with anything close to a straight face that this problem was exclusive to China. The corporate parent received the benefits from any profits made due to the bribery so it is difficult to image why a corporation should not be a part of any enforcement action. I suspect that both the DOJ and the SFO will be asking the dreaded *"Where Else"* question about now.

The GSK tale drives home the point that having a compliance program is useless unless it is effective. Further, it is clear that by putting such an affirmative defense in place, companies may well go the paper compliance defense route and not dedicate the time and resources to make it effective. So whether you were pro or anti-compliance defense, I think that GSK is a stand-in for the Grim Reaper and what the matter will portend in this brave new world of global anti-bribery and anti-corruption enforcement.

Chapter XXII - China and the International Fight Against Corruption

GSK may well be a watershed in the global fight against bribery and corruption. Behavior and conduct, which was illegal under Chinese law but previously tolerated and even accepted by Chinese government officials, quickly became a quagmire that the company was caught in when charges of corruption were leveled against them last year. Many westerners were skeptical about the claims made against GSK and its head of China operations, Mark Reilly. That is one of the problems in paying bribes to government officials; it is always illegal under domestic law. David Pilling, writing an article in the FT, entitled *"Why corruption is a messy business"*, said "Multinationals are discovering that there is only one thing worse than operating in a country where corruption is rampant: operating in one where corruption was once rampant – but is no longer tolerated."

When it began, it was not it clear why China's Communist Party Chief Xi Jinping began his anti-corruption push. Some speculated that it was an attack on western companies for more political reasons that economic reasons. Others took the opposite tack that the storm, which broke with the bribery and corruption investigation of GSK, was China's attack on western companies to either hide or help fix problems endemic to the Chinese economic system. My take is that his campaign has a different purpose but incorporates both political and economic reasons. That purpose is that Xi has recognized something that the US government officials and most particularly the DOJ have been preaching for some time. That is, the insidiousness of corruption and its negative effects on an economic system.

Xi and China have realized that corruption is a drain on the Chinese economic system. Publications as diverse as the Brookings Institute to the WSJ have noted that one of the reasons for the anti-corruption campaign is to restore the Chinese public's faith in the ruling Communist Party. Bob Ward, writing in the WSJ article entitled *"The Risks in China's Push to Root Out Wrong"*, said, "China's anticorruption drive began in late 2012 as a way to cleanse the ruling Communist Party and convince ordinary Chinese that the system isn't rigged against them. Investigators are targeting some of China's most powerful officials and disciplining tens of thousands of lower-echelon officials who party investigators contend got used to padding their salaries." Cheng Li and Ryan McElveen, writing online for Brookings, in an article entitled *"Debunking Misconceptions About Xi Jinping's Anti-Corruption Campaign"*, wrote, "If there were ever any doubts that Xi could restore faith in a party that had lost trust among the Chinese public, many of those doubts have been dispelled by the steady drumbeat of dismissals of high-ranking officials since he took office."

But the economic reasons behind the anti-corruption campaign are equally important. One of the more interesting articulations came from one disgraced former Chinese government official, who was one of the earliest senior officials to be charged with corruption. In a WSJ article by James T. Areddy, entitled *"Chinese Ex-Official Admits to Corruption"*, he wrote about the trial of Liu

Tienan, the "former head of the National Energy Administration and senior director in the National Development Reform Commission" who had been arrested in May 2013. His trial finally came around in September 2014. At his trial he made some rather extraordinary statements. Areddy wrote, "Liu testified that reducing official power is key to curbing corruption: "The major point, which is based on my own experience, is to give the market a great deal of power to make decisions."" But Liu did not end there, "as he explained his view that China's state bureaucracies are too powerful and entrepreneurs are too weak. "Approvals should be developed in a system, rather by an individual's actions. This would help prevent abuse of power for personal self-interest.""

Whether or not Liu thought those statements up on himself, a smart defense lawyer suggested he make them to reduce his sentence, or the Chinese government told him to say it as his role in the well-known show trials of the Chinese justice system; it really does not matter. That is one of the most incredible statements I have ever heard of coming out of anything close to an official Chinese statement or proceeding. Think about it; first Liu is saying that the Adam Smith's 'invisible hand' of the market should be governing market decisions. Next, he speaks against the arbitrary nature in China for entrepreneurs in giving approval about how businesses can expand and grow in China. This arbitrary process should be replaced with objective criteria. It is almost if Lui is channeling his inner FCPA Professor when he speaks against artificial barriers to market entry. Finally, Liu attacks the small-mindedness of bureaucratic mentality in their use of power for self-interest.

There have already been demonstrated economic benefits to China's anti-corruption campaign. In September, Bloomberg reported that China's fight against bribery and corruption could boost economic growth, generating an additional $70 billion for the budget, in summarizing economists' forecasts. An article in the online publication Position and Promotions, reported that the bribery "could trigger a 0.1-0.5 percent increase in the world's second-biggest economy, equivalent to $70 billion dollars." This crackdown should also be welcomed by western companies, as "it could also benefit foreign companies operating on the Chinese market, who have experienced the negative effects of the omnipresent palm-greasing, according to Joerg Wuttke, president of European Chamber of Commerce in China." He was further quoted as saying, "It takes the stress away. You're not afraid that somebody gets an order because he found a better champagne or something like that. It's not Singapore yet, but it's a very positive development".

As we close this phase of GSK's bribery and corruption saga in China, I think some time for reflection is appropriate. For the compliance practitioner there have been many specific lessons to be learned from GSK's missteps. However I think the clearest lesson is that the only real hope that a company has in today's world is an effective, best practices anti-corruption compliance program. Whether it is designed to help a company comply with the FCPA, UK Bribery Act or other anti-corruption legislation, really does not matter. It is the only, and I mean only, chance your company will have when an issue in some far-flung part of the world splashes your company's name across the world's press.

But there may also be cause for celebration to those who have long preached against the evils of corruption, whether it is for economic reasons or for those who view the fight against anti-corruption as a part of the fight against terrorism. For if China is attacking domestic corruption, I believe that will lead other countries to do so as well. We are already seeing stirrings in India under new President Modi. So while GSK may well suffer going forward, the fight against global bribery and corruption may just have moved a few feet forward.

About the Author

 Thomas Fox practices law in Houston, Texas. He is the author of two internationally award winning books dealing with anti-bribery and anti-corruption: *Lessons Learned in Compliance and Ethics* and *Best Practices Under the FCPA and Bribery Act.* His most recent book, *Doing Compliance*, was published by Compliance Week in October 2013. He is the Managing Editor of the award-winning *FCPA Compliance and Ethics Blog* and is a Contributing Editor to the FCPA Blog, a Contributing Writer to Compliance Week, is a featured contributor to Corporate Compliance Insights (CCI) and is a Columnist for SCCE Magazine. He is the author of numerous articles on the FCPA, UK Bribery Act and compliance and ethics. He is also an internationally recognized speaker in the field of anti-bribery and ant-corruption compliance. He can be reached at tfox@tfoxlaw.com.

www.ingramcontent.com/pod-product-compliance
Lightning Source LLC
Chambersburg PA
CBHW070931180526
45168CB00003B/1032